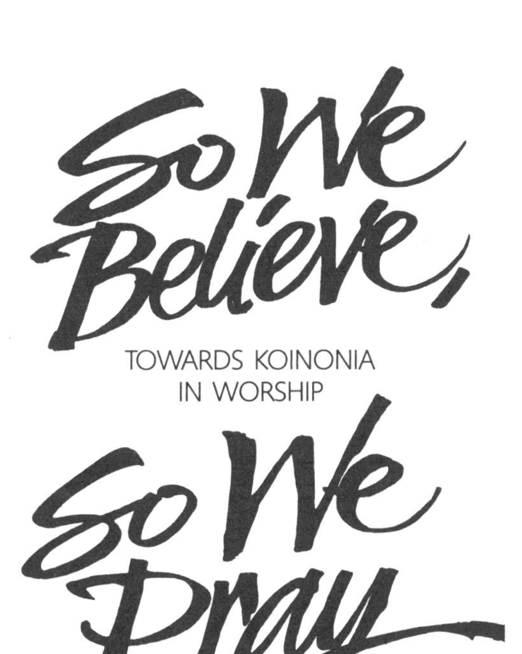

TOWARDS KOINONIA
IN WORSHIP

Edited by
Thomas F. Best and Dagmar Heller

Faith and Order Paper No. 171
WCC Publications, Geneva

Cover design: Stephen Raw

ISBN 2-8254-1159-0

Printed in Switzerland

Table of Contents

III. The Worship Life of the Consultation

A. SERMONS

B. ORDERS OF WORSHIP

IV. Participants, Contributors

Preface

Prayer and Unity. By a Layman (most probably the honorary secretary and jurist Robert H. Gardiner) — this official brochure no. 15 of the Faith and Order movement referred (already in 1913) to the fundamental significance of worship, prayer and spirituality for the emerging efforts towards Christian unity. The insight that common prayer and worship anticipate, express and prepare experiences of Christian communion that both reflect and stretch beyond theological agreements and convergences has informed the work of the Faith and Order movement (since 1948, the Commission) from its early stages.

For nearly seventy years Faith and Order has been closely associated with the Week of Prayer for Christian Unity. The world conferences on Faith and Order in 1952 at Lund and 1963 at Montreal both dealt in one of their sections with the relationship between worship and the unity of the church. In 1969 a consultation was held on "Worship in a Secular Age". Worship and prayer were integral elements of Faith and Order's studies leading to the document (1982) on *Baptism, Eucharist and Ministry* (BEM). The so-called "Lima-liturgy" has exercised a strong influence on ecumenical worship life. Faith and Order was very much involved in the preparation of the ecumenical hymn book *Cantate Domino* (1947) and the two editions of the Ecumenical Prayer Cycle *For All God's People* (1978) and *With All God's People* (1989). And there are the annual meetings with the Pontifical Council for Promoting Christian Unity to prepare the material for the *Week of Prayer for Christian Unity*.

Yet despite all these activities it was felt and suggested on many sides that Faith and Order should reflect once again, in a more explicit and direct way, on the interrelation between common worship and the theological efforts towards full communion: worship as an expression of the koinonia we already share, and worship as impulse and as source of strength on the way towards koinonia in its fullness. A strong request in this sense came especially from the fifth world conference on Faith and Order at Santiago de Compostela, Spain, in 1993. This was indeed appropriate as the world conference itself laid great stress on its daily life of prayer and Bible study as fundamental to its work for visible unity.

The response to these requests was the consultation on the theme "Towards Koinonia in Worship" held at Ditchingham, England, in August 1994. We are happy that the report and papers from this extremely important and fruitful consultation are now made available to a broader audience. These texts contain a wealth of theological insights and practical suggestions. These will be taken up in the ongoing studies of the

Faith and Order Commission. But their significance for other ecumenical efforts is equally obvious. Indeed, we hope the publication of this material will help to inspire further contacts between Faith and Order and the community of liturgists and others active in the field of worship.

We are very grateful to the Rev. Janet Crawford, the moderator of the consultation; to the Rev. Dr Thomas Best for carrying major staff responsibility for the consultation and this publication, together with his colleague the Rev. Dr Dagmar Heller and the WCC worship consultant the Rev. Terry MacArthur; and to Mrs Eileen Chapman for her work as administrative assistant for the meeting, Mrs Béatrice Bengtsson for her earlier preparatory work, Ms Monica Schreil for her assistance with this publication, and Ms Renate Sbeghen for her help with proofreading.

Commission on Faith and Order
Geneva, December 1994

Mary Tanner, Moderator
Günther Gassmann, Director

Introduction

> We are divided from one another not only in matters of faith, order and tradition, but also by pride of nation, class and race. But Christ has made us His own, and He is not divided. In seeking Him we find one another.[1]

Many Christians taste the truth of this statement most immediately and powerfully in the experience of Christian *worship*. In seeking Christ in worship together with Christians from various confessions and from all the world over, they experience "glimpses of unity, foretastes of full koinonia".[2] Many testify that it is such experiences that give them the strength to continue in the search for unity and in acts of common prophetic witness and service. Surely there are difficult moments, and deep hurt, as when Christians are unable to eat together at the table of the Lord. Yet even such moments may inspire us to work all the harder to resolve those divisions which keep us eating and drinking at our separate tables. *For we are not the only ones who desire our unity:* the Spirit itself hungers and thirsts for our unity, and the Spirit's desire is unquenchable, and finally it will prevail.

Towards Ditchingham

That is the conviction, the passion, which has inspired this book and the meeting which produced it. In August 1994 a group of liturgists, theologians, church musicians and local pastors, from all over the world and from most of the major Christian confessions, a group both diverse and competent, brought together at an Anglican community of Sisters at Ditchingham, near Norwich, England, by the Faith and Order Commission of the World Council of Churches, fashioned together a meeting on the role of worship within the search for Christian unity. This book records the presentations and written results, as well as something of the experience, of the remarkable week which we spent together. Because our own worship as a community was integral to our life and work together, these materials are included as well. Thus we make here available, in addition to the Letter and Report from the consultation (which have been in circulation since soon after the meeting[3]) a full documentation of the event, including all the written sources which directly undergirded and nourished our reflection.

The meeting sought to bring together crucial developments over the past thirty years in two fields: first, in the study and practice of Christian worship, both in the particular churches and in ecumenical contexts; and second, in theology, specifically ecumenical reflection on the nature and life of the Christian church and its calling to unity. Indeed it was perhaps the first *common* exploration, by a group representing both these fields, of the landmark developments in each, of their inter-relation and mutual significance, and of their implications for the unity of the church.

In the area of worship, recent years have been marked by a profound liturgical renewal, supported by a flourishing of liturgical scholarship. We have noted above the growing experience of worship in ecumenical contexts. On such occasions Christians from different confessions, meeting for prayer and reflection, have joined together in worship which expresses — as authentic worship does — Christ's universal gift in terms appropriate to the actual community gathered in that place.

But liturgical renewal has also marked the lives of particular churches. Seeking a renewed openness to the Spirit, recovering anciently-attested worship patterns, encouraging the production and use of new hymns, rediscovering the importance of baptism within the whole of the Christian life, re-emphasizing the central importance of preaching and the eucharist, including the more frequent and regular celebration of the supper — all these have brought a new vitality to the worship life of many churches.

In the area of theology, equally significant developments have occurred. Exploring converging convictions about such central matters as baptism, eucharist and ministry, documenting the sources of division in these and other areas in order to move beyond them, exploring the relation of church unity to the unity of the human community, joining in common witness and service in face of the needs of the world, seeking a common witness on issues of justice, peace and the integrity of creation, and asking about the significance of such developments for the unity of the church — all these testify to the theological progress made by the churches together in the final third of this "ecumenical century".

What has been missing in ecumenical reflection, however, is the link *between* these developments in worship and in theology. There has been too little theological reflection about these developments in worship practice, and their implications for the unity which we seek. And theological reflection on the nature of the church, its life and its unity, has drawn far too little upon what should be one of its formative sources, namely what is actually being experienced in worship, both in particular churches and in ecumenical contexts. As one liturgist noted during our meeting:

> Liturgical scholars... are frequently surprised when they discover theologians still struggling over issues which belong to other pastoral times and seem appropriate only to radically different forms of the liturgy than those celebrated today.[4]

In short: the *lex orandi* and the *lex credendi*, the "rule for prayer" and the "rule for belief", have tended to become separated in the ecumenical discussion, not to mention in the lives of many churches. The vital connection between the two "rules" has become weak; and the practice of theology and the practice of worship are not each nourishing the other as they should. This was the situation which the Ditchingham meeting sought to address.

Towards koinonia in worship: some results from Ditchingham

The various materials here collected speak for themselves and need no special introduction. We would like, however, to point to four areas which were central to our gathering, and in which the results of our common prayer and reflection may prove particularly useful to the churches and within the ecumenical movement.

The first area is the notion of the *ordo*, a "common ordering and scheduling of the most primary elements of Christian worship".[5] Many churches, in pursuing their own process of liturgical renewal, have discovered a convergence towards fundamental patterns of Christian worship. Such a resource — rooted in the New Testament, witnessed to in the sources of the ancient church, practised increasingly, and with more conscious intention, among more and more churches today, and capable of wide variations in local practice — can be a powerful inspiration for unity. It provides a basis for Christians and the churches, while exploring new possibilities in worship, to remain accountable to the experience of Christians through the ages. By offering a touchstone, it helps the churches to appreciate each other's distinctive gifts and emphases in worship.

The second area is that of inculturation, how worship expresses the universal faith in cultural forms appropriate to each particular place. This is a complicated process, involving both respect for local cultures and, where necessary, their critique. Faithfully done, it "tends towards the unity of the churches in essentials of faith; and it serves as an instrument of evangelization".[6] At Ditchingham we noted afresh the role of inculturation in worship as a powerful force for *local unity*: the different local churches, originally transplanted from abroad, tend to grow together in adopting local cultural forms to express the universal Christian faith. It was no accident that we linked the process of inculturation to the WCC Nairobi assembly's vision of "local churches truly united..."[7] The ecumenical implications of this have yet to be discerned.

The third area is the lifting up of ways in which worship is already actively fostering the search for unity. Thus while our work flourished through formal reflection upon issues of worship and unity, it was rooted in many and varied examples of worship life in specific local situations. We heard how Christians in Latin America and Africa are expressing the one faith in cultural forms appropriate to those places; and we explored how the riches of a particular tradition, for example the Orthodox use of icons, may contribute to the worship experience of other churches within the ecumenical movement. We heard how in united churches worship undergirds the coming together of separated church bodies into one; how in church union negotiations theological agreements are put into liturgical form, thus bringing them most effectively into the life of local congregations; how local ecumenical projects — "ecumenical parishes" bringing together various traditions — shape worship which expresses their commitment to common confession, witness and work.

The fourth area is the question of how Faith and Order itself can address issues of worship in relation to unity, and how the dimension of worship can be brought into its own life and its work for the unity of the church. A generous set of specific suggestions is offered in the report.[8] These need not be repeated here, but we want to stress our conviction that Faith and Order spoke rightly in saying at Louvain (1971):

> ...in all Faith and Order studies the importance of considering the subject in close relation to its expression in worship should continually be remembered. Indeed sometimes such expression may form basic material *without which the study cannot yield fruitful results*.[9]

The dimension of worship is both intrinsic and *essential* for Faith and Order's future work towards the unity of the church.

Continuing concerns

Besides these points we mention five concerns which have sparked special interest, and which also call for further reflection and action. One concern is the need of those within the ecumenical movement to have spiritual resources adequate to their task. That is, in addition to public assembly for worship we need to nourish the practice of personal prayer, Bible reading and meditation. One of our proposals, then, is for a "rule for ecumenists", "a discipline of prayer or other patterned spiritual practice, which would nourish them in the search for unity and remind them to do all things with charity".[10] We hope this proposal can be taken up widely in many areas of the ecumenical movement.[11]

A second concern is the need to develop more fully the relationship of worship to work for justice, witness and service, to the Christian commitment that God's will be done "...on earth as it is in heaven". All our deliberations at Ditchingham would affirm this connection,[12] and there was general and clear assent to the following statement from one of the liturgists among us:

> Christian worship is a sharp critique to a world that regards material progress as the ultimate aim of history... at the same time we Christians are invited by the liturgy to involve ourselves in the human struggle for justice, peace and true progress.[13]

Strikingly this issue has also begun to be addressed in Faith and Order's work on the relation of ecclesiology and ethics.[14] A fruitful collaboration could certainly be developed at this point.

A third concern is the relation of our work to those whose worship is not characterized by formal structure, and where the "free play of the Spirit" has a much greater role, as well as to churches which understand worship in other than "sacramental" terms. While our work speaks freely, as is proper, of the sacraments and of form in worship, we do not understand this as denying the need for freedom and experimentation in our assemblies. We reminded ourselves that there are different "styles" of worship, and urged one another to welcome the gifts which diverse worshipping communities can bring to our understanding of worship.[15] But we recognize that much needs to be done to bring "sacramental" and "non-sacramental" churches together for common reflection. Progress here would be helpful to the ecumenical movement as a whole, for this issue is related to a wide range of questions such as the use of creeds, the function of symbols in theology and worship, and not least the question of the structure of the church and its ministry.

We found ourselves drawn again and again to the urgency of work on two of the central and formative aspects of Christian worship, namely baptism and the eucharist. This needs now to be pursued with a new awareness of their liturgical as well as theological dimensions.

Thus a fourth concern is the need for further work on baptism as the event which initiates us all into the one body of Christ. The Ditchingham report offers *Baptism, Eucharist and Ministry*[16] as a model of the "discussion of classic points of division in the light of shared liturgical patterns", with baptism taken as a particular example.[17] The point is sharpened in the conclusion of the report, where we urge the churches to draw more actively the implications of our "increasing mutual recognition of one another's baptism as the one baptism into Christ".[18] Faith and Order now foresees work on a baptismal *ordo*; the elements of this are increasingly present in the worship of many churches, and such a liturgical convergence could nurture and help express the growing theological convergence in this area.[19]

A fifth concern is the need for further work on the eucharist, the table at which Christ desires that we sit together to sup with him. We rejoiced together that their common understanding of faith and sacramental life enables an increasing number of churches to practise eucharistic fellowship with one another. We noted the experience of many Christians and churches over recent years in using the "Lima liturgy",[20] an unofficial Faith and Order text which seeks to embody in liturgical form the theological convergences recorded in BEM.[21] In other cases, of course, substantial and complex differences remain, and there we faced seriously the fact of our inability to sit down together at the table of the Lord.[22] We urge further reflection on the lessons to be learned from the widespread use of the Lima liturgy, as well as a broader discussion of the current possibilities for eucharistic worship in ecumenical contexts.[23]

Concluding comments

It remains to record our thanks to the Community of All Hallows and its leader Mother Pamela, and to all those who made us feel so welcome and who did so much to support our coming together. We were blessed and empowered through meeting in a community which holds worship visibly at the centre of its own life. As organizers of the meeting we also extend our thanks to Mrs Eileen Chapman and the other staff members (they are named on p.viii above) who did so much on behalf of our work.

We want also to invite reaction and response to the material in this book. It is offered as an impulse to discussion, both within the churches and ecumenically, about the central role of worship in the search for Christian unity. Readers' comments will be warmly welcomed and these may be addressed to Dr Thomas F. Best or Dr Dagmar Heller at Faith and Order, Unit I, World Council of Churches, 150 route de Ferney, 1211 Geneva 2, Switzerland. We would also be happy to provide information about further Faith and Order work related to worship, particularly in the fields of baptism and eucharist.

At Ditchingham we explored fundamental things, things central to our experience of Christian worship and to our search for Christian unity. We found that these central things are also, perhaps far more than we have realized, *common* things. If we are (to use a word of Julian of Norwich) "avid" for Christ and for our unity in him, then these common things of worship will be precious resources for our drawing together towards our final unity in Christ. If we value Christ above all else, above even our own divisions, then these things will be dear to us, and if they are, then through them Christ will draw us to himself. In seeking Christ in worship — in *finding* Christ there, and *being found by* him — we approach the Centre of all things. And in finding that common centre we shall surely find each other.

Thomas F. Best
Janet Crawford

Dagmar Heller
Terry MacArthur

NOTES

[1] "The Message of the Assembly", *The First Assembly of the World Council of Churches*, ed. W. A. Visser 't Hooft, London, SCM, 1949, p.9.

[2] "Report of the Consultation", para. 47, p.16 below.

[3] The Letter has been published in *ENI Bulletin*, no. 2, 26 September 1994, pp.25-26, in *The Ecumenical Review*, vol. 47, no. 1, January 1995, pp.104-105, and in *Ökumenische Rundschau*, vol. 1, January 1995, pp.104-106; the letter and report have been published in *One in Christ*, vol. XXXI, no. 1, 1995, pp.71-73 and 73-100; the letter and report (minus appendices) in *Studia Liturgica*, vol. 25, no. 1, 1995, pp.1-3 and 3-31; the report in *Mid-Stream*, vol. 34, no. 2, April 1995, pp.197-229.

[4] Gordon Lathrop, "Knowing Something a Little: On the Role of the *Lex Orandi* in the Search for Christian Unity", note 8, p.48 below.

[5] "A Letter on Koinonia in Worship", p.3 below, and report, para. 4, p.6 below.

[6] Report, para. 36, pp.12-13 below.

[7] Report, para. 8, p.7 below.

[8] Paras 43-64, pp.15-21 below.

[9] Report, para. 49, p.16 below. The quotation is from the report of committee II on "Worship Today", 5, in *Faith and Order, Louvain 1971: Study Reports and Documents*, Faith and Order Paper No. 59, Geneva, WCC, 1971, p.281, emphasis added.

[10] Report, para. 58, p.18 below.

[11] An effort which is more broadly aimed but includes specific suggestions in this area is the "Envoys for Ecumenism" programme of the Massachusetts Council of Churches. Further information is available from the Council at 14 Beacon Street, Boston, MA, 02108-3760, USA.

[12] Para. 9, p.8 below.

[13] "Liturgical Inculturation and the Search for Unity", by Anscar J. Chupungco, O.S.B., p.60 below.

[14] See "Ecclesiology and Ethics: A Reformed Perspective", by Duncan Forrester, *The Ecumenical Review*, vol. 47, no. 2, April 1995, pp.148-154. For example: "When Karl Barth published his Gifford lectures... some English-speaking readers were surprised to discover, in a book which they assumed was about the relation between theology and ethics, substantial discussions of the cultic service of God (*Gottesdienst*) alongside the treatment of the political service of God...", p.149.

[15] "Knowing Something a Little: On the Role of the *Lex Orandi* in the Search for Christian Unity", by Gordon Lathrop, p.40 below.

[16] *Baptism, Eucharist and Ministry*, Faith and Order Paper No. 111, Geneva, WCC, 1982.

[17] Report, para. 11, p.8 below.

[18] Para. 67, pp.21-22 below. The quotation was used at Ditchingham in the mid-day worship for 22 August 1994 (see p.130 below); it comes originally from the daily worship for 9 August 1993 from Santiago de Compostela (see the *Worship Book: Fifth World Conference on Faith and Order, op. cit.*, p.12.

[19] Indeed such a study was broached in one of our presentations. For example: "In other words, across their confessional differences the churches share certain elements that constitute a baptismal *ordo*." See "Liturgical Inculturation and the Search for Unity", *op. cit.*, p.62 below. (Significantly this affirmation was supported by a listing of seven such "elements" from the fourth world conference on Faith and Order at Montreal in 1963.)

[20] "The Eucharistic Liturgy: Liturgical Expression of Convergence in Faith Achieved in Baptism, Eucharist and Ministry", Geneva, WCC, 1983, reprint of appendix II of *Ecumenical Perspectives on Baptism, Eucharist and Ministry*, ed. Max Thurian, Faith and Order Paper No. 116, Geneva, WCC, 1983, pp.225-246.

[21] *Baptism, Eucharist and Ministry*, Faith and Order Paper No. 111, Geneva, WCC, 1982.

[22] Report, paras 13-17, pp.8-9 below.

[23] At a recent Lima liturgy workshop held at the Ecumenical Institute, Bossey, one group continued the discussion reflected in Appendix I of the Ditchingham report, pp.22-24. The resulting text, "Celebrations of the Eucharist in Ecumenical Contexts", is published in *The Ecumenical Review*, vol. 47, no. 3, July 1995 and elsewhere, and is available directly from Faith and Order. The members of the group, principally from Anglican, Lutheran, Reformed and Free Church traditions, offer the text as a stimulus to wider ecumenical discussion.

I

Towards Koinonia in Worship: The Ditchingham Letter and Report

A Letter on Koinonia in Worship

26 August 1994

To Christians, as they care about the unity and the worship of the churches,

From the members of a consultation on the role of worship in the search for Christian unity, held at Ditchingham (near Norwich), England, and convoked by the Commission on Faith and Order, Programme Unit I (Unity and Renewal), World Council of Churches:

Dear Sisters and Brothers in Christ:

"May mercy, peace and love be yours in abundance" (Jude 2).

Gathered here, from many churches and nations of the world, in the hospitality of the sisters of All Hallows Convent, we have been moved to write to you of the urgent matters in which we have found profound agreement.

In the divided world, marked by massive injustice, bitter warfare and vast sorrows, the churches of Jesus Christ remain visibly divided. These are the very Christians for whom Jesus prayed when he asked that those who believe in him through the apostolic word might all be one "so that the world might believe" (John 17:21). Generations of Christians have joined that prayer, though they have sometimes grown weary of praying or even indifferent to the search for Christian unity. We wish to shake off the indifference in ourselves and arise from the weariness. Will you, in your place, join us?

Here in Ditchingham, we have seen the body of Christ in the presence of each other — Roman Catholic, Orthodox, Anglican, Lutheran, Reformed, Baptist, Methodist, Disciples of Christ, Mar Thoma, United and Uniting Church Christians, from local churches in Africa, Asia, Europe, Latin America, North America and Oceania. We have been moved to hear of many instances in local places where visible koinonia between and in the churches is emerging. We give praise and thanks to God, believing that the prayer for unity is being answered.

But we also believe that Jesus Christ himself, crucified, risen and present in our midst, is the eternal answer to the prayer. We are one as we dwell in him and as, through him, the Holy Trinity dwells in us. We must become, visibly, what, in his mercy, we already are.

For this drawing near to Christ, communal assembly for worship is essential. Indeed, for being Christ's body visible in each place, for koinoinia between and in the churches, for being the church at all — worship is essential. And we have been finding, to our joy and astonishment, that we share together, as our common inheritance, the deepest gifts of worship: the gospel of Jesus Christ, the great patterns of Christian gathering in the truth of that gospel, the call to see those patterns celebrated in ways appropriate to the dignity and gifts of each local place, and the conviction that this celebration sends us in a mission of love and the search for justice in the world.

May we ask you to join us

— in renewed prayer for the unity of the churches, such as Christ wills and by the means that Christ wills;
— in a new and deeper study of the sources and meaning of Christian corporate worship;
— in a commitment to clarify and renew our local worship so that our witness to the world and the grounds of our koinonia may be shown forth by the centrality of these common gifts: Sunday assembly, scripture reading, preaching, intercessions, thanksgiving at the holy table, eating and drinking the gift of Christ, forming new Christians in the faith and praying for them, baptizing, and sending in mission to the world;
— and in a decision to undertake this prayer, study and renewal together with other Christians, across our divisions?

We have in common these holy things of worship: baptism, the word, eucharist, prayer, assembly, the celebration of the resurrection on Sunday and at *Pascha*/Easter. These things are dear to us, and were at the heart of our discussions in Ditchingham, not only because we share them but because in them we encounter Christ and in him, in the power of the Spirit, we come to the Father. In them we are given a foretaste of the world reconciled in God's love. In them we are given each other. In them we are formed to stand with the poor and suffering ones of the world. Together with you, we all, in these holy things, are given Jesus Christ, "the bread of God which comes down from heaven and gives life to the world" (John 6:33).

Join us, we ask you.

O God, holy and eternal Trinity,
we pray for your church in all the world.
Sanctify its life; renew its worship;
empower its witness; heal its divisions;
make visible its unity.

Lead us, with all our brothers and sisters,
towards communion in faith, life and witness
so that, united in one body by the one Spirit,
we may together witness to the perfect unity of your love.
Amen.

Towards Koinonia in Worship: Report of the Consultation

Introduction

> The fruit and end of our prayer is to be made one with our Lord
> and to live for him in all things
>
> Julian of Norwich
> Revelations of Divine Love, Chapter 42

In August 1994, 32 Christians from all over the world brought together in Ditchingham (near Norwich), England, many different experiences of pilgrimage. Our reflection on the place of worship in the search for unity at the invitation of the Faith and Order Commission of the World Council of Churches was shaped by prayer itself. The vision of Mother Julian of Norwich from the past met us and inspired us towards God's glorious promise.

We were well blessed, living for a week in the Community of All Hallows, Ditchingham, under the loving hospitality of devoted sisters in Christ. They shared with us their quiet practice and steeped us in the daily office, whilst graciously permitting us to offer our unfamiliar gifts to them as we celebrated within their midst Christian practices from many cultures and traditions.

This colourful variety yielded to a cohesive form. Within the giving and receiving *we held together* experiences of the unity of worship without which any appreciation of koinonia would be impaired: church *and* world; word *and* sacrament; gospel *and* creation; Christ *and* culture; life *and* faith. We recognized that we need one another across the spectrum of Christian memory and cultural experiences and that we are actually part of the growth towards koinonia in worship.

In the middle of the week we were given a poignant sign of this pattern and blend. We had just visited the site of Julian's cell and worshipped in Norwich cathedral when the quintessential nature of the English summertime afforded us the sight of a vivid rainbow. The rainbow elicits a holistic view, since, although its colours may be strong and distinctive, none is isolated from the rest. All blend together, each receiving from and offering to the spectrum, the resultant light being glorious.

So it is, we believe, about our koinonia in worship. There are many strong, distinctive aspects from varied backgrounds. We are not all the same, nor are we made to be;

except that what we are is part of a wholeness that is infinitely greater than our monochrome singularity. We need each other to reflect that and we need to be *together* for God's glory to shine fully in the world. For, like the rainbow, we too are called to reflect the light.

That is the message of this report, throughout which the pattern of pairing appears not because it has been artificially superimposed but because this was *our* discovery of what is given and required.

In the biblical and theological foundations of our koinonia in worship we have identified, in place of a haphazard scattering of unrelated stones, building blocks fitting together, "mutually reinterpretive juxtapositions, roots in word and sacrament held together" (paragraph 4, below). Building on this are "characteristic pairings" (10) which help to clarify things that have divided us when they should have united us in faith and practice — such as baptism and the eucharist. So we see koinonia which is "renewed and enlivened" (19) both by expressions of perceived truth *and* the experience of praying together and using common worship resources — the process of reconciliation through the healing of memories. The gospel is then related to life, transforming cultural components by integrating them in worship, taking care over "dynamic equivalence" (37).

Such "pairs" of experience continuously reflect upon each other like colours in the rainbow, belonging together in a pattern. When, therefore, we come finally to note the relationship of our koinonia in worship to the agenda of Faith and Order we are suddenly surprised by the obvious, like the rainbow in the sky, as if it were conceivable that faith and order could *ever* have been studied independently of our worshipping together (45). So we dare to suggest some fresh perspectives on the totality of faith and order, as if, having seen the glory of the promise of God, we cannot help but share what we have experienced.

Was not this, put another way, what Mother Julian discovered as she prayed and then offered the fruits of her experience to others? As freely as we have received from the gracious hand of God, we humbly offer to the end that our experience at prayer may issue in our oneness in the Lord that we live for him in all things.

I. Biblical and theological foundations

1. "Blessed be the God and Father of our Lord Jesus Christ! By his great mercy he has given us a new birth into a living hope through the resurrection of Jesus Christ from the dead" (1 Pet. 1:3).

Blessed be God's great love which has already given to us the holy koinonia for which we pray through the one baptism into Christ Jesus, which continually founds and forms all the churches.[1] Beyond our expectation, God has given us that koinonia as we all, together, being "buried with Christ by baptism into death", are raised with him day after day "by the glory of the Father, so we too might walk in newness of life" (Rom. 6:4). That koinonia has been given to us in the common life of the believing community, which is empowered with many gifts by the Holy Spirit, which eats and drinks the "holy communion" of Christ, and which shows forth a foretaste of the communion of the whole creation with God, a foretaste of all peoples reconciled to

God and to each other through the cross and resurrection of Jesus Christ.[2] The gift we have received is also our calling and task. The koinonia we seek between and within the churches is a koinonia in and through Jesus Christ. It is a participation in the grace and eternal life of God for the sake of the life and salvation of the world.[3] "God is faithful, by whom you were called into the fellowship of his Son, Jesus Christ our Lord" (1 Cor. 1:9).

2. This crucified and risen Christ, the ground and source and centre of our koinonia, is alive today in our midst. Koinonia is found in the scriptures opened to speak of him to our burning hearts (Luke 24:13-32), in the broken bread and cup of blessing which are a participation in the body and blood of Christ (1 Cor. 10:16), and in the one Spirit in which "we were all baptized into one body" of Christ (1 Cor. 12:13).[4] Word and sacraments, signs of the presence of Christ, are set forth in the midst of a participating assembly of people who are gathered by the Spirit, blessed with many different gifts, and sent to bear witness with their lives to the same love and mercy of God for all the world which has been shown forth in their assembly.

3. Through the coming of the Spirit, Christian worship is thus a continual meeting with Christ, so that we might be gathered into the grace and life of God. Many different Christian traditions enrich us as we think of the meaning of this encounter. It is a speaking of the gospel of Christ so that we might come to faith. It is grace flowing from the sacrifice of Christ. It is the beginning of the transfiguration of all things in the Spirit of Christ. It is a gift and call for personal holiness according to the measure of Christ. It is the visible manifestation of the incarnation of Christ so that we might be formed in incarnational living amid the "sacrament of the world". It is beholding Christ in the gathering so that we may be able to behold him and love him among the marginalized, outcast and disfigured ones of the world. It is the participation in the Spirit-led meeting as "baptism" and in every shared meal as the "Lord's supper". It is praise and thanksgiving to the Father through Christ in the unity of the Spirit. But all these understandings depend upon Christian worship being centred in the encounter with God in Jesus Christ through the power of the Spirit enlivening the word and the sacraments. And all these understandings presuppose that this encounter occurs in an assembly which is itself a witness to God's intention with the world and which forms its participants for a life of witness and service. The liturgy of Christians occurs in assembly: it also occurs in the midst of daily life in the world (see Rom. 12:1-2).

4. The pattern of this gathering and sending has come to all the churches as a common and shared inheritance. That received pattern resides in the basic outlines of what may be called the *ordo* of Christian worship, i.e. the undergirding structure which is to be perceived in the ordering and scheduling of the most primary elements of Christian worship. This *ordo*, which is always marked by pairing and by mutually reinterpretive juxtapositions, roots in word and sacrament held together. It is scripture readings and preaching together, yielding intercessions; and, with these, it is *eucharistia* and eating and drinking together, yielding a collection for the poor and mission in the world. It is formation in faith and baptizing in water together, leading to participation in the life of the community. It is ministers and people, enacting these things, together. It is prayers through the days of the week and the Sunday assembly seen together; it is observances through the year and the annual common celebration of the *Pascha* together. Such is the inheritance of all the churches, founded in the New Testament, locally practised

today, and attested to in the ancient sources of both the Christian East and the Christian West.

5. This pattern of Christian worship, however, is to be spoken of as a gift of God, not as a demand nor as a tool for power over others. Liturgy is deeply malformed, even destroyed, when it occurs by compulsion — either by civil law, by the decisions of governments to impose ritual practice on all people, or by the forceful manipulation of ritual leaders who show little love for the people they are called to serve. At the heart of the worship of Christians stands the crucified Christ, who is one with the little and abused ones of the world. Liturgy done in his name cannot abuse. It must be renewed, rather, by love and invitation and the teaching of its sources and meaning. "And I, when I am lifted up from the earth, will draw all people to myself," says Jesus (John 12:32). The liturgy must *draw* with Christ, not compel.

6. Furthermore, this pattern is to be celebrated as a most profound connection between faith and life, between gospel and creation, and between Christ and culture, not as an act of unconnected ritualism nor anxious legalism. Every culture has some form of significant communal assembly, the use of water, speech which is accessible but strongly symbolic, and festive meals. These universal gifts of life, found in every place, have been received as the materials of Christian worship from the beginning. Because of this, we are invited to understand the Christian assembly for worship as a foretaste of the reconciliation of all creation and as a new way to see all the world.

7. But the patterns of word and table, of catechetical formation and baptism, of Sunday and the week, of *Pascha* and the year, and of assembly and ministry around these things — the principal pairs of the Christian liturgy — do give us a basis for a mutually encouraging conversation between the churches. Churches may rightly ask each other about the local inculturation of this *ordo*. They may call each other towards a maturation in the use of this pattern or a renewed clarification of its central characteristics or, even, towards a conversion to its use. Stated in their simplest form, these things are the "rule of prayer" in the churches, and we need them for our own faith and life and for a clear witness to Christ in the world. And we need each other to learn anew of the richness of these things. Churches may learn from each other as they seek for local renewal. One community has treasured preaching, another singing, another silence in the word, another sacramental formation, another the presence of Christ in the transfigured human person and in the witnesses of the faith who surround the assembly, another worship as solidarity with the poor. As the churches seek to recover the great pairs of the *ordo*, they will be helped by remembering together with other Christians the particular charisms with which each community has unfolded the patterns of Christian worship, and by a mutual encouragement for each church to explore the particular gifts which it brings to enrich our koinonia in worship.

8. This pattern or *ordo* of Christian worship belongs most properly to each local church, that is, to "all in each place".[5] All the Christians in a given place, gathered in assembly around these great gifts of Christ, are the whole catholic church dwelling in this place. As efforts are made to enable local occasions of ecumenical prayer and as local churches are clarifying the full pattern of Christian worship as the centre of their life, a groundwork is being laid for local unity. "Local churches truly united"[6] will be one in faith and witness, and, amid continuing diversity of expression, one in the practice of the most basic characteristics of the *ordo*. This same pattern or *ordo* of

Christian worship is a major basis for the koinonia between local churches, a koinonia spanning both space and time, uniting churches of the New Testament times, of the sweep of Christian history and of the present oikoumene. Such a koinonia can only be enriched by those authentic forms of inculturation which the *ordo* may have taken in each local church, not diminished.

9. The factors described above along with the renewal of many other dimensions of the churches' worship life have led communities to a deepened sense of koinonia and to rediscover the relationship between their worship and the active fulfilment of their baptismal mission. It does not yet appear what our koinonia in Christ may be. But we know that as we faithfully gather around word and sacrament, signs of the living Christ and of the power of the Spirit, as we faithfully see their connections to all of life, and as we share the sufferings of a church which longs for unity and a world which longs for justice, we participate in an icon of that future which God's great love and mercy is bringing towards all the world. We pray for that future and we already begin to receive it and to become part of it. And, bearing witness to the aching and needy world, we sing praise to the One whose mercy is everlasting and whose faithfulness endures to all generations.

II. Building on the foundations

10. In the ongoing discussion of many of the ancient issues which have divided us, the above pattern or *ordo* of Christian worship is immensely helpful. Much clarity may be obtained when discussions about the age appropriate for baptism, about the nature of ordained ministry, about the sacrifice of Christ and the sacrifice of Christians, and about social justice are seen in relationship to the pattern of worship and its characteristic pairings.

11. The *Baptism, Eucharist and Ministry* document[7] is itself a model of such discussion of classic points of division in the light of shared liturgical patterns. Thus, for example, when baptism is seen to be a process of both faith-formation and water-washing, believer baptist groups may be able to see themselves as enrolling their young children in a catechumenate, recognizable to many other Christians, while infant-baptizing groups may find their own life-long call to discipleship and learning refreshed, and both groups will find themselves called to a strong celebration of baptism which shows forth its centrality and meaning.[8] Future Faith and Order discussions could well be formed according to this model, with liturgical studies a welcome partner in the conversation.

12. Although there have been many positive responses to the BEM text and also bilateral agreements on baptism resulting in some changes in practice, yet there is much work still to be done. In addition to the use among some of the churches of a shared certificate of baptism, further possible steps are the celebration of baptism in common during the Easter vigil, or the joint construction and use of a common font/ baptistery. We also realize that much of what has been accomplished in the area of mutual recognition of baptism is put at risk by churches diverging from the traditional formulae for the administration of baptism in the use of water in the name of the Father and of the Son and of the Holy Spirit.

13. With regard to the eucharist, many Christians have come to see that participation in the holy supper is a participation in the one, undivided Christ. They also remember

that Jesus welcomed all, without distinction, to eat with him. Some Christians then feel called by God to an immediate openness at the table, to as wide a practice of hospitality at the eucharistic table as possible. Others believe that without the deepest agreement in the apostolic faith and without a fully shared local church life, this mutual eucharistic hospitality is not yet possible. Both groups feel the pain of our divisions. We have felt that pain here, at Ditchingham. But Christ is one, and he is our only source of unity. As we eat and drink from him in the eucharist we nonetheless participate in each other. We need now to continue to ask what that participation means for the development of renewed local churches in full communion with other local churches.

14. We rejoice at the growing sharing of communion between Christians, a growth encouraged by changes in church rules and by exposure to ecumenical contacts. At the same time we acknowledge the increasing impatience of many where such sharing is not possible. This was expressed powerfully by the then general secretary of the World Council of Churches, Emilio Castro, who said at the seventh assembly of the WCC at Canberra in 1991:

> It is more and more frustrating that this [eucharistic sharing] has not been realized. We are able to be together in confronting the most divisive problems of humankind, but we are not able to heal our own history and to recognize each other within our common tradition... How can we expect to overcome divisions of life and death in the world when we are not even able to offer together the sacrifice of the Lord for the salvation of the world?[9]

15. We welcome the statement in the recent report of the consultation on "Christian Spirituality for Our Times" (Iasi, Romania, 1994) which said:

> For the centrality of the eucharist is not only a tradition in the majority of our churches, but one of the fruits of spiritual renewal together. The desire for a common eucharistic celebration and sharing arises from the sense of community and koinonia in Christ experienced when members of different churches engage together in the struggle for justice and peace, or commit themselves to shared mission, ministry and witness.[10]

16. We also endorse the recommendation of the Iasi consultation to the WCC

> that fresh efforts be made towards, and new guidelines be proposed on, eucharistic sharing in time for the eighth assembly of the WCC; this would take into account current ecumenical relationships and experiences, the churches' current canonical regulations and the ecclesiology on which these are based, and the degree of doctrinal convergence on baptism, eucharist and ministry, and on the apostolic faith today.[11]

17. Another help to mutual understanding and respect would be for the churches to act upon the suggestion made at Santiago de Compostela:

> We suggest that the churches, while respecting the eucharistic doctrine, practice and discipline of one another, encourage frequent attendance at each other's eucharistic worship. Thus we all will experience the measure of communion we already share and witness to the pain of continued separation. Furthermore, those various expressions of ordinary hospitality which do form part of our liturgies must not be perfunctory gestures, but genuine expressions of Christian affection for each other.[12]

18. The very *ordo* or pattern itself outlined in paragraphs 4 to 8 above needs a continued ecumenical clarification. Besides the work already done on baptism,

eucharist and ministry, the churches need to address the renewal of preaching, the recovery of the meaning of Sunday and the search for a common celebration of *Pascha* as *ecumenical* theological concerns. This last is especially urgent, since an agreement on a common date for Easter — even an interim agreement — awaits further ecumenical developments. Such an agreement, which cannot depend on the idea of a "fixed date of Easter", should respect the deepest meaning of the Christian *Pascha*, the Nicene decision, the traditions of both East and West, the date of Passover, and the feelings of Christians throughout the world. We welcome all initiatives which offer the hope of progress in this important area.

III. Expressing and fostering koinonia in worship

19. In worship Christians are able to express the koinonia that unites them and at the same time to find that koinonia nourished and strengthened. For it is only as the Christian community together draws nearer to God the Father in common allegiance to Jesus Christ and in the power of the Holy Spirit that its own koinonia is renewed and enlivened.

20. In the history of Faith and Order, as the Montreal world conference (1963) indicated, there has been strong emphasis on the importance of worship in the ecumenical movement and for theological work in general. It described worship as "the central and determinative act of the church's life".[13] It also laid stress on "the Trinitarian basis of worship and its fundamental ecclesiological relevance".[14] The centrality of worship in the life of the church was also affirmed in the Constitution on the Liturgy, *Sacrosanctum Concilium*, of the Second Vatican Council which spoke of the eucharist as the source and summit of the life of the church.[15]

21. The Second Vatican Council also issued a decree on ecumenism, *Unitatis Redintegratio*, which said:

> Church renewal... has notable ecumenical importance. Already this renewal is taking place in various spheres of the church's life: the biblical and liturgical movements... all these should be considered as promises and guarantees for the future progress of ecumenism.[16]

The Roman Catholic experience following Vatican II with the opportunity for worship in the vernacular and the emergence of the charismatic movement within that church has opened up similar exciting developments in worship in many parts of the oikoumene.

22. At the same time, the fuller participation of the Orthodox churches in the life of the World Council of Churches in the 1960s brought a new perspective into the life of the Council and of its member churches.

23. Since the 1960s there have been significant changes in worship in the churches, and a growing awareness of the catholicity of the church as the ecumenical movement has continued to bring together Christians of different countries and cultures. Many of those

> who once could not even say a prayer together can now celebrate their faith and join in significant acts of worship (e.g. sharing in the Week of Prayer for Christian Unity, in the

> World Day of Prayer, in the Week of Prayer for [World] Peace, in joint Bible studies and using the common Ecumenical Prayer Cycle).[17]

We affirm that

> through such common prayer and a meeting of minds and hearts on a deeper spiritual level, many are experiencing an "ecumenical conversion", which strengthens at the same time their rootedness in their own tradition and opens them to the insights and riches of the wider Christian community.[18]

24. During this same period there developed in some places local congregations of Christians from two or more confessions uniting for mission and sharing a common worship life (for example the Local Ecumenical Partnerships in Great Britain and the Cooperating Parishes in Aotearoa/New Zealand). In their own localities they have found it possible to overcome historic divisions on baptism, eucharist and ministry and thus to share fully in eucharistic worship.

25. These developments happened in a period when liturgical renewal was undergirded by developing theological convergences. These convergences were encouraged by the study of BEM and by the results of a number of bilateral dialogues.

26. Theological convergence, liturgical renewal, and the recognition of the indissoluble relationship between worship and mission in Christ's way, are all part of the momentum driving the churches towards koinonia in worship.

27. Not only do Christians pray together, they also increasingly use common worship resources. Whereas for a long time music for worship flowed mainly from Europe to other parts of the world, now there is a greater mutual sharing between the continents. Music from Africa, Asia and Latin America greatly enriched the World Council of Churches' assemblies at Vancouver (1983) and Canberra (1991) as well as many other gatherings, including the fifth world conference on Faith and Order (1993), and is now part of the normal diet of worship in many congregations where it was once unknown. The Eastern and Oriental Orthodox churches have also made a significant contribution to the musical resources of the ecumenical movement. The communities of Taizé and Iona have had an influence in many places. The charismatic movement also has contributed a new repertoire of songs and a new musical style.

28. Among some churches there is a movement towards the development of common lectionaries. Through these, Christians are rediscovering their common "ownership" of and mutual responsibility for the proclamation of the scriptures. There is also a growing agreement about the churches' observation and celebration of the liturgical year and many are using ecumenical prayer cycles such as *With All God's People*.[19] We welcome the projects of the Consultation on Common Texts, the Joint Liturgical Group and the English Language Liturgical Consultation[20] and encourage further work towards an ecumenical lectionary and calendar.

29. There is now much greater sharing of spiritual and cultural gifts between Christians in their worship. For the Orthodox the place occupied by icons in holy worship expresses the reality of koinonia, for "icons are a witness that the human being, called to live in Christ and the Holy Spirit, is to become a participant in the divine nature" (2 Pet. 1:4).[21] Today icons are coming to play an increasingly important place in the life of prayer of many Christians. Also many have found that the

koinonia which they share is expressed and nurtured as they join with those traditions which practise retreats and pilgrimages, and discover new spiritual texts for private devotional use.

30. Liturgical scholars, working from common sources, have come closer to a common sense of the *ordines* for baptism, the eucharist and daily prayer. Working with these findings, the renewed liturgies of many churches have a common shape which creates a sense of common heritage of worship among the churches. Often, texts (particularly eucharistic prayers) from our common past, notably those from Hippolytus and Basil of Caesarea, have once again become living texts within the regular worship of liturgical assemblies.

31. In many places ecumenical committees work together to produce common worship texts for use in the churches as well as common services for pastoral occasions such as baptisms, weddings and funerals.

32. Not only does the use of common liturgical material foster reconciliation among Christians, but also new liturgies specifically of reconciliation and healing of memories have been, and are being, written and used with effect. For example the churches in Ireland, through the work of such bodies as the Irish School of Ecumenics and the Corrymeela community, have done some solid work in developing and using such liturgies.

33. While we rejoice in these developments and the renewal that has come with them, we recognize that our koinonia is still imperfectly realized, and there are ecclesiological questions which are yet to be resolved. The question of sharing in one eucharist will not be solved by a text (such as the Lima liturgy), but by theological agreement on eucharist and ministry. In some local situations some practises have gone beyond the level of official theological agreement, thus implying assents to matters of ministry and sacrament which have not been given formally.

34. It also must be acknowledged that although common prayer and worship can and do unite Christians across deep divisions, we cannot be complacent. Communities which have shared common worship and prayer may break down into communal violence, as recent events in the former Yugoslavia and in Rwanda have shown. Such tragic events reveal that our koinonia may indeed be fragile.

IV. Koinonia and the inculturation of worship

35. It has already been made clear that worship must be both authentic to the gospel and Christian tradition, and relevant to life. In the quest for authenticity, the relationship between worship and culture is of particular importance. The task involves identifying premises, discerning principles and setting criteria. Interdisciplinary study is necessary.

A. PREMISES

36. Inculturation is a form of creative activity accountable to both received liturgical tradition and the actual praxis of the church as well as to the integrity of culture; it tends towards the unity of churches in essentials of faith; and it serves as an instrument

of evangelization. Cultural diversity of local churches expresses the richness of the entire koinonia. Their worship mirrors the unity and catholicity of the church. At the same time, inculturation enhances the koinonia of local churches across confessional lines by bringing about a closer cultural resemblance among them in worship.

37. Among the different methods of inculturation, that of dynamic equivalence merits particular attention, because it is partial to the preservation of unity. It consists of re-expressing components of worship with something in the local culture that has an equal meaning or value. In this way inculturation leads to the diversity of cultural expressions within the unity of tradition.

38. Certain observations need to be made regarding culture, namely: that God can be encountered in culture; that Christ awaits to be discovered in every culture; that sinfulness also exists in culture; and that hence the church is called to evangelize culture in order to bring out more fully the presence of Christ.

B. PRINCIPLES

39. Liturgical inculturation operates according to basic principles emerging from the nature of Christian worship, which is

a) trinitarian in nature and orientation;
b) biblically grounded; hence the Bible is one indispensable source of worship's language, signs and prayers;
c) at once the action of Christ the priest and of the church his people; hence it is a doxological action in the power of the Holy Spirit;
d) always the anamnesis of the mystery of Jesus Christ, a mystery which centres on his death, resurrection, the sending of the Holy Spirit, and his coming again;
e) the gathering of the priestly people who respond in faith to God's gratuitous call; through the assembly the one, holy, catholic, and apostolic church is made present and signified;
f) a privileged occasion at which God is present in the proclaimed word, in the sacraments, and in the other forms of Christian prayer, as well as in the assembly gathered in worship; and
g) at once remembrance, communion and expectation; hence its celebration expresses hope of the future glory and dedication to the work of building the earthly city in the image of the heavenly.

40. In the process of inculturation it is important to consider seriously also those principles that are inherent in the church's liturgical tradition, e.g. baptism is normally administered during public worship, and eucharist is celebrated every Sunday.

C. CRITERIA

41. Liturgical inculturation should observe the following criteria:

a) *Theological criteria* based on the *lex orandi* of biblical and apostolic tradition. This tradition refers to the word of God consisting of reading and preaching in the power of the Holy Spirit; baptism with water in the name of the Father and of the Son and of the Holy Spirit; eucharist as the ritual "breaking of bread" in memory of Christ who died and rose for us; the community of believers and its ministers; and social concern flowing from the eucharist.

These theological criteria are rooted in the mystery of Christ's incarnation, which is the model of liturgical inculturation, and in the mystery of his death and resurrection whose living presence in the world is the ultimate goal of liturgical inculturation.

b) *Liturgical criteria* based on the elements constituting the shape of the liturgy which the churches received in full or in part. These elements refer to baptism, eucharist, and the other forms of public worship such as the service of the word, and the prayer of the hours (morning and evening prayers and vigils).

   i) The basic liturgical components of baptism that emerge from tradition are: proclamation of the scripture; invocation of the Holy Spirit; renunciation of evil; profession of faith in the Holy Trinity; and the use of water in the name of the Father and of the Son and of the Holy Spirit.

   ii) The usual liturgical components of the eucharist are: the reading and preaching of the Lord; intercession for the whole church and the world; and, in accord with the actions of our Lord at the last supper, taking bread and wine to be used by God in the celebration; blessing God for creation and redemption; breaking the bread; and giving the bread and the wine. Tradition includes the recitation of the words of institution and the invocation of the Holy Spirit at the eucharistic prayer, and the recitation of the Lord's prayer.

   iii) The question regarding the use of bread and wine for the eucharist is a sensitive one that needs to be examined closely in the light of scripture, history, theology and culture.

   iv) The basic liturgical components of the service of the word that emerge from tradition are reading from scripture, preaching or exposition of the word, and intercessions for the church and the world.

   v) These components are part of liturgical tradition and should be preserved and transmitted through inculturation. History tells us, however, that a number of liturgical components developed in the course of time through contact with local cultures. While respecting the basic components of Christian worship, the process of liturgical development should remain active even today.

   vi) Worship not only involves texts and rites but also music, liturgical space, and cycles of time. All of these should be shaped according to the criteria of liturgy and the requirements of local culture.

c) *Cultural criteria* based on the components of culture. These are human *values* such as family, hospitality and leadership; the people's *patterns* of language, rites and the arts; and *institutions* such as rites of passage and festivals. These are the things with which worship holds dialogue and hence should be closely examined. Cultural elements for integration into the liturgy should possess a "con-natural" quality to express the meaning and purpose of Christian worship. That is why, while churches should respect what is honest, noble and beautiful in every culture, not everything good in culture is necessarily suited for the liturgy. Furthermore cultural elements should not remain as tokens or as alien bodies that do not relate to Christian worship.

It should, however, be acknowledged that some cultural components have been infected by sin, and hence need critique. Critique presupposes both correction and transformation of those cultural components which are integrated into Christian worship. Critique can sometimes involve a break with such cultural elements as are diametrically opposed to the gospel. Critique can also mean that Christian worship has a counter-cultural dimension.

D. SOME NECESSARY TASKS

42. In order to engage fruitfully in the work of liturgical inculturation, we need to examine the received traditions and actual praxis of our own church and how they relate to those of the other churches of the Christian koinonia. Likewise we should explore the nature of inculturation together with its dynamics and methods. Lastly we need to study our own local cultures with their values, patterns, and institutions, and how they can suitably be integrated into Christian worship after due consideration and critique.

V. The aspect of worship within the work of Faith and Order

43. The church is by its very nature a worshipping community. It exists to praise God, to give thanks to God for God's manifold gifts to creation and to his people, and to invite others to take their place within this circle of celebration. Its worship prefigures that final worship when "every creature in heaven and on earth and under the earth and in the sea, and all that is in them" will bow before God's throne, singing to the Lamb "blessing and honour and glory and power, for ever and ever" (Rev. 5:12-13).

44. All reflection upon the church and its nature, purpose and mission must touch on the reality of worship, for it is in worship that the church both experiences and expresses the deepest source of its life. When it is at worship the church is whole and it is one.

A. THE IMPORTANCE OF WORSHIP FOR FAITH AND ORDER

45. Therefore exploring the experience and meaning of worship, and the role of worship within the churches' search for visible unity, is an essential aspect of the work of Faith and Order. According to its by-laws the aim of Faith and Order is

> to proclaim the oneness of the church of Jesus Christ and to call the churches to the goal of visible unity in one faith and one eucharistic fellowship, *expressed in worship* and in common life in Christ, in order that the world may believe.[22]

This is why Faith and Order is mandated to promote "prayer for unity",[23] and why one of its functions is "to study such questions of faith, order *and worship* as bear on this task".[24] (It should be clear that the "study" of worship does not mean a merely rational or theoretical analysis, for that would be foreign to the nature of worship itself.)

46. Christians long for the day when they can manifest fully the oneness which God has given them in their common baptism into Christ. They are avid for the day when finally they can sit together at the one table of their one Lord. Much patient work has been done, not least by Faith and Order, in exploring the theological and ecclesiologi-

cal issues which continue to divide the churches. And when those differences have been overcome, it will be through acts of worship, especially baptism and the eucharist, that our full koinonia will be experienced, celebrated and made visible to the world. As expressed by the statement "The Unity of the Church as Koinonia: Gift and Calling" adopted by the World Council of Churches seventh assembly in Canberra (1991):

> The unity of the church to which we are called is a koinonia given and expressed in the common confession of apostolic faith; a common sacramental life *entered by the one baptism* and *celebrated together in one eucharistic fellowship*...[25]

47. Yet even in our present divided state we experience and manifest glimpses of unity, foretastes of full koinonia, in the many common acts of worship in which Christians are already able to join. This is a witness to the astonishing growth in the relationships among Christians and the churches in this ecumenical century.

48. This growing experience of worship with other Christians is directly relevant to the churches' search for visible unity. Many Christians have found that it is through worship with Christians of other traditions that they are most empowered to continue their work for visible unity. And often it is through worship that theological agreements are most effectively brought into the life of the churches, as convergence in doctrine and practice is expressed and experienced within the context of the community gathered in prayer and in praise of God. As one section at Santiago de Compostela said:

> [We recommend] that Faith and Order develop strategies and initiatives for promoting the reception on local and national levels of ecumenical agreements, being aware that reception has also a spiritual dimension. This may include... encouraging churches to employ these agreements, whenever appropriate, in prayer life and worship...[26]

49. Historically Faith and Order has recognized the need to include the aspect of worship within its reflections on theological and ecclesiological issues. For example, the Commission meeting at Louvain (1971) was convinced that

> in all Faith and Order studies the importance of considering the subject in close relation to its expression in worship should continually be remembered. Indeed sometimes such expression may form basic material *without which the study cannot yield fruitful results*. We have in mind in particular any future studies on catholicity, on the preparation of a common declaration of faith, on the unity of mankind in relation to social questions, and to the diversity of races and cultures.[27]

The final sentence indicates the extraordinary range of issues for the study of which the Commission thought a sensitivity to worship was essential. We are convinced that this approach is even more important today. All that has happened in and through the ecumenical movement since Louvain — and much *has* happened since Louvain — underscores the need to bring the theme of worship once more into the work of Faith and Order.

B. THE ASPECT OF WORSHIP IN RELATION TO FUTURE FAITH AND ORDER WORK

50. The programme of Faith and Order through the next (eighth) WCC assembly is outlined in the "Conspectus of Faith and Order Studies 1994-1998"[28] agreed by the Standing Commission at its meeting in Crêt-Bérard in January 1994. This includes:

a) a focal study on ecclesiology, drawing together the results of recent Faith and Order work, the experiences of the united and uniting churches, bilateral discussions, and other factors;
b) several (six have been proposed) independent, specialized studies whose results will also contribute to this work;
c) cooperative work within Unit I of the WCC on worship and spirituality (the Ecumenical Pilgrims project, the Ecumenical Prayer Cycle), and with other units in the fields of gospel and culture (Unit II) and ecclesiology and ethics (Unit III); and
d) four long-standing programmes, including the Week of Prayer for Christian Unity and three others (in connection with the united and uniting churches, bilateral dialogues, and the Joint Working Group) through which Faith and Order relates to particular aspects of the one ecumenical movement.

51. Our reflections at this meeting have shown that worship is linked in important ways to all of these themes, and that paying attention to the dimension of worship would significantly enhance all of these studies. To put it more sharply: without the dimension of worship the studies might yield (in the language of Louvain) "fruitful results", but those results would be partial and perhaps distorted because this integral aspect of the being and life of the church has not been taken into consideration.

C. FRESH PERSPECTIVES FOR FAITH AND ORDER

52. We indicate below various specific studies, and ways in which the dimension of worship could be addressed within each. But before this three general points must be raised, for they touch on the orientation and style of Faith and Order work as a whole.

1. Regional perspectives

53. Faith and Order has shown its commitment to listen more carefully to the distinctive perspectives of the churches in the various regions of the world. Our work at this consultation has shown that the issue of inculturation in and through worship must be part of this process. Through this issue we touch, for example, the following themes:
a) Authenticity and identity: how can the apostolic (authentically Christian) faith be expressed "in each place" in forms which are integral to local culture and respectful of local identity?
b) Translating vs transplanting: authentic *translation* of the Christian faith into the "language" of local cultures allows it to be appropriated by those "in each place". Sadly the Christian faith has often come by a process of *transplantation* which has confused the content of the faith with the cultural forms in which it is brought.

54. As persons "in each place" gather in worship they present themselves, rooted as they are in a particular time and place, before God who is the Lord of all time and all space. Through a valid process of inculturation all that is good in each culture may become a vehicle for the praise of God. This means that in listening more carefully to the regions Faith and Order must take serious account of their worship life, and not only their formal theological statements. This might involve a systematic study of how worship life is shaped in the various cultures.

2. Communication: verbal and non-verbal

55. Within worship, words interact with manifold non-verbal forms of communication. All the senses may be brought to the service of praising God and all may be vehicles through which God is present among the worshippers. Through sight and song, through dance, through touch, through smell and taste the presence of God is communicated. The worship space itself plays an important role in this process. There is a special place for silence and stillness in worship.

56. Has the "verbal ethos" of Faith and Order, its focus upon the written word as the bearer of theological meaning, limited its understanding of worship and its importance in the search for Christian unity? If Faith and Order is to engage the issue of worship seriously, it must become more sensitive to visual settings and non-verbal forms of communication.

57. This suggests that Faith and Order should explore new means of communicating with a wider audience. The exposition of the Roublev icon of the Trinity at the WCC Vancouver assembly by Bishop Dr William Lazareth (then director of Faith and Order) and Metropolitan Daniel of Moldavia and Bukovina, later produced by Faith and Order as a videotape and widely used in some churches, shows that it is possible for Faith and Order to work creatively in this area.

3. Spiritual ecumenism

58. "Spiritual ecumenism" refers to the source of our common commitment to the goal of visible unity. This must be a life of worship, Bible study, prayer and spiritual discipline which keeps us going in the face of all obstacles and apparent lack of progress. Only within such a broader spiritual context can we forgive one another time and again as we cause pain through misunderstanding or insensitivity. Could the commissioners of Faith and Order discern on the basis of their own spiritual practice, or that of their communities, a "rule" for those active in the ecumenical movement, a discipline of prayer or other patterned spiritual practice, which would nourish them in the search for unity and remind them to do all things with charity?

D. WORSHIP IN RELATION TO SPECIFIC FAITH AND ORDER STUDY PROGRAMMES

1. The church as koinonia — an ecumenical study (the focal "ecclesiology study")

59. This study must incorporate the dimension of worship in its reflections upon the nature of the church and its unity. We have noted these topics:

a) How worship expresses the nature of the church, and how in worship we experience the reality of the church (through both verbal and non-verbal forms of communication).
b) The relation between the theological positions of the various churches and their expression in worship (further comparative study of worship forms and content may be needed).
c) The question of unity and diversity as expressed within worship: what are the criteria for authentic worship practices? How can we enable the practices of particular ecclesial communities to enrich the wider church?

d) What is the place and role of the worship which we offer together in our ecumenical gatherings? How does it relate to the worship of the various churches? (This is related to the wider question of the ecclesial significance of ecumenical meetings and bodies.)
e) Is there a "sacrament of presence" which we offer to one another as we attend one another's worship? Can our very presence — even when we cannot participate fully — be understood as a form of "intercommunion"? What does this say about questions of sacramental sharing? Should we put greater emphasis upon those many bonds of communion through which we are given real but still incomplete unity?
f) A process of inculturation raises profound issues of unity and catholicity. Authentic inculturation often leads to common forms of worship (as well as common theological perspectives) which express a certain unity at the local level. How does this relate to the unity of the church universal? How does it relate to the various traditions or communions of churches to which the different local churches belong?

2. Towards koinonia in worship

60. In this consultation we have begun to explore how the dimension of worship is central to the churches' search for greater visible unity. Many expressed a concern that the work of the consultation be continued for it has become evident that questions of faith and order can hardly be studied independently of worship. The following points among others were noted during the presentations and discussions (cf. also the recommendations, below):

Programmatic work

a) There should be further study of the *ordines* (i.e. the basic pattern and structural elements) of Christian worship. We see here an emerging ecumenical convergence which both expresses and nurtures our path "towards koinonia in worship".
b) There should be further study on inculturation as an exercise of "accountable creativity", and its relation to the unity of Christians "in each place". This could involve collaboration with the Lutheran World Federation worship and culture study.
c) There should be further study of specific examples of how churches and Christians are expressing in worship the koinonia which they already enjoy. These may well offer important learnings for other churches and for the whole ecumenical movement.
d) Appropriate initiatives should be encouraged in such areas as the work for a common date for Easter, possible revision of the guidelines for eucharistic services at ecumenical meetings, further work on liturgical expressions (appropriate to different cultural settings) of the convergences reached in *Baptism, Eucharist and Ministry*, and efforts to renew and broaden the observance of the Week of Prayer for Christian Unity.

Faith and Order contacts

a) Contacts should be developed with liturgists, theologians with special sensitivity to liturgical issues, and worship leaders. This could involve distributing the report and news of this meeting to liturgical journals, including liturgists as participants in Faith and Order meetings, and ensuring a Faith and Order presence at meetings of groups such as the Societas Liturgica.

b) Consideration should be given in filling places on the Faith and Order Commission to liturgists and theologians with special sensitivity to liturgical issues, as well as worship leaders.

3. Apostolicity and apostolic faith today

61. These issues are pertinent:

a) The historic creeds are frequently used today within the context of worship; this use has developed and changed over time. They are not simply theological statements (Zizioulas, Santiago de Compostela[29]). Any study of the creeds should include their role within the worship life of the church. Their "meaning" must be explicated with that context in mind.

b) Faith and Order is currently developing a short "study guide" from the apostolic faith study programme. This text should be sensitive to the role of the creed within worship. Could the text itself, or another document, include worship materials?

4. Ministry and authority

62. Issues of ministry and authority are closely related to the worship life of the churches, and to possibilities for common worship among Christians from different traditions. (To take an example from ecumenical experience, difficulties with full participation in the Lima liturgy often arise over the authority of the president. This can be the case even when there is agreement on the text itself.) In light of the relation between these issues and worship:

a) In considering the positions of the various churches on ministry and authority, the study should address questions such as the following: Who may exercise leadership in worship? What roles are appropriate in worship for clergy and lay persons? What kind and extent of participation in worship is appropriate? Who decides in such matters?

b) The study should consider the implications for worship of convergences which are reached on issues of ministry and authority.

c) The study should be sensitive to how lack of agreement on issues of ministry and authority hampers our ability to worship together.

5. Ecumenical hermeneutics: interpreting and communicating the one faith in koinonia

63. The following points are pertinent:

a) Of all the many languages it is the "language" of worship which is particular to the church. The study of hermeneutics must embrace not only theological texts but also worship and how the faith is experienced and expressed in the context of worship.

b) The study should embrace the wide range of Christian symbols and forms for experiencing and communicating the faith. How can we help all Christians to be nourished by forms precious to particular traditions (icons, for example), so that these can bring Christians together?

c) Different traditions have profoundly different understandings of symbolic forms, and of particular symbols. What is precious to some may seem irrelevant or even unacceptable to others, and sometimes Christians have destroyed symbols of faith precious to other Christians. How can we foster mutual respect and understanding?

6. Unity of the church and nationalism and ethnic identity

64. Worship is a powerful means through which Christian communities express not only their Christian faith but also their cultural identity. This study would benefit from considering the following issues:

a) How is the relation between Christian identity and national/ethnic identity expressed in worship (comparative study may be necessary here)?
b) How can our *worship* remind us that as Christians we belong to a worldwide faith that transcends all other belongings and loyalties?

VI. Conclusion

65. We were reminded early in our meeting of the challenge which the churches posed themselves at the third world conference on Faith and Order at Lund in 1952:

> Should not our churches... act together in all matters except those in which deep differences of conviction compel them to act separately?[30]

Much progress has been made, not least in the field of worship. We have been encouraged by the growing recognition of a pattern for Christian worship shared by the churches as their common inheritance, and by our explorations of how the one gospel of Jesus Christ can be celebrated by those "in each place". We have rejoiced to hear how in worship Christians are expressing and experiencing that degree of koinonia which they already enjoy. And we have been heartened to see how through worship the results of theological agreements are being experienced within the lives of the churches, thus nurturing their search for unity.

66. And yet we know that in worship, as in other areas (as acknowledged in the World Council of Churches Canberra assembly statement "The Unity of the Church as Koinonia: Gift and Calling"),

> churches have failed to draw the consequences for their life from the degree of communion they have already experienced and the agreements already achieved.[31]

We know also that where serious theological differences remain between the churches, it is often in worship that they become most immediately — and painfully — visible. Thus despite progress in implementing the Lund principle much remains to be done towards that day when we can experience and express in worship that full koinonia which is ours within the one body of Christ.

67. In our own worship in Ditchingham we affirmed and celebrated together (as at the fifth world conference on Faith and Order) "the increasing mutual recognition of one another's baptism as the one baptism into Christ".[32] But how far have Christians and the churches drawn the implications of that common baptism, that common belonging

to the one body of Christ, for worship? The words of Lund continue to challenge us: how far *have* the churches consistently and seriously applied them in their worship? What difference would it make if they *were* seriously applied?

Recommendations

By general affirmation the plenary agreed the following:

1. We recommend that the report of this consultation be transmitted to the Faith and Order Standing Commission for its consideration and use.
2. We recommend the publication of this report with the papers and other related documents so as to make the work of this consultation more widely available. We strongly recommend that the material be translated into other languages.
3. We recommend the translation of the "Letter to All Christians" into other languages to enable as wide a distribution of this text as possible.
4. We recommend that the findings of this consultation be transmitted to the appropriate bodies for consideration in the process of preparing worship material for major WCC meetings, e.g. the mission conference (Salvador, Brazil, 1996) and the eighth assembly (Harare, 1998).

Appendix 1: The Lima Liturgy

[In response to widespread interest a discussion group met at Ditchingham to study the forms, use and future role of the "Lima liturgy". An account of the group discussion was presented in plenary. The following text resulted from this process.]

1. The group noted its origin as a liturgy which was inspired by the theological work of the BEM document, and was used at the 1982 meeting in Lima of the Faith and Order Commission where that document was finalized. It was drafted by one distinguished scholar and ecumenist and adapted by a small group for use at that meeting. By the time it was first published,[33] it had already been refined and edited for wider use.

2. The original text has been adapted for use at other great ecumenical occasions, notably the WCC assemblies at Vancouver and Canberra. Significant changes to the original text were made for these celebrations, particularly to include the theme of the meeting or occasion. Our group noted that greater adaptation could take place: there has been a tendency to accept the original version somewhat automatically or uncritically when used for a local or regional gathering. But the Lima liturgy was not intended to remain in fixed form: the commentary by Frère Max Thurian indicated ways in which it might be adapted and abbreviated for other uses.[34]

3. Many, indeed, have commented on the wordiness of the Lima liturgy. It may perhaps be more appropriate for grand occasions (we note that length is a culturally relative matter!) but the words have been carried by the work of musicians and artists available at the WCC assemblies. Without these gifts, the Lima text is often too formal and too complex for many local events.

4. Nevertheless, it has proved valuable in many other contexts, from regional councils (e.g. the Christian Conference of Asia meeting at Seoul in 1985), national ecumenical occasions (we were told of its use in Kenya), and in Local Ecumenical Partnerships

(such as the one at Milton Keynes, UK). It clearly has had a catechetical value, and has offered an accessible model of eucharistic worship to many churches.

5. These groups would be helped, however, by a publication which re-edited the original Lima version in the light of its later adaptations, and included a commentary which indicated when and how other appropriate changes might be made. That is, it might be prepared as a kind of *editio typica*, using Lima as an example, and intended to encourage its contextualization.

6. However, the ecumenical movement needs to build on what it has through Lima, and draw into its discussion the wisdom of the wider liturgical movement. It is clear that the original Lima liturgy was but *one* attempt to order the eucharistic celebration in the light of the BEM process. Paragraph 27 of the Eucharist section (E.27) of BEM, which lists the elements of a eucharistic liturgy, interestingly lists them in what could be the structure of an actual celebration. The original Lima liturgy itself differs from this list at some significant points. (E.27 does point out that the elements may occur in another sequence, and that they are of differing importance.) Our group thought that E.27 needs to be brought into primary place in the discussion, and that together with the insights we have received at Ditchingham on the *ordo* and inculturation, it ought to be the framework for preparing a number of local adaptations of the original Lima liturgy. BEM itself does not envisage a single structure or pre-determined content for a eucharistic liturgy. The Lima version of the Lima liturgy needs to be seen in a wider perspective.

7. It ought also to be noted that the Lima liturgy is received chiefly as a printed text. It is the work of theologians; it was intended in part to celebrate particular doctrinal convergences. There are dangers in this: it may lead us away from the primary purpose of any liturgy, the worship of God. The main purpose of liturgy cannot be catechesis. A liturgy cannot be too closely tied to a particular theme, even theological themes like baptism, eucharist and ministry. Its one theme is that of the scripture: the work of God through Christ in the Holy Spirit for which we give thanks. The Lima form also has the danger of over-clericalization: lay leadership needs more careful designation.

8. There are also wider questions to do with this exercise in itself: should the WCC be involved in preparing a eucharistic liturgy (or, taking in the full sweep of BEM, baptismal liturgies and ordinals)? Certainly the ecumenical movement has moved on in the last fifty years or so from simply inviting fellow-Christians to attend the characteristic celebration of a particular host church.[35] The confessional element remains, of course, in that the presider or president of the liturgy must have the authority of a particular church, and on that the participation of others depends. At the end of this ecumenical century however, such presiders on ecumenical occasions, while they may use some elements distinctive of their own tradition, will also likely draw on the large pool of liturgical and musical resources which are now accepted across the churches (and nations and cultures). This is a new relationship between the confessional and the ecumenical in prayer and worship.

9. The presider (and/or committees preparing for worship) may also apply "confessional" theological principles in the adaptation of the Lima liturgy itself. This has already happened (we think) in recent versions of the Lima eucharistic prayer. That prayer, for instance, does reflect the emerging ecumenical convergence, but at the same time it must be said that it sits much more comfortably within the recent Roman

Catholic liturgical framework. It does use elements familiar in other traditions, e.g. the epiclesis (invocation of the Spirit) from the Eastern churches, but in a Roman way (i.e. it is a "consecratory epiclesis"). It is important to note that not only the elements, but also their place in the liturgy, has theological import. Structures will thus be more or less ecumenically acceptable according to their implied sacramental theology. Another example is the peace, which is in a place closer to where it appears in a Roman Catholic liturgy, and not where it is familiar to Eastern churches, or in recent Anglican and Reformed liturgies which use it, i.e. as the hinge between the service of the word and the service of the sacrament.

10. It must also be clearly faced that the Lima liturgy (or any other "ecumenical eucharistic liturgy") does not and cannot deal with the question of who may receive holy communion. It is a liturgy which can only be used by those churches who may authorize the use of liturgical forms other than their own. Roman Catholic and Orthodox Christians are still unable to participate fully in such a eucharist, and "ecumenical" is rather too large a claim to make. This is not to say that the search for ways to celebrate liturgically the unity we have received should not continue: quite the opposite. We need to place high value on our sharing of the liturgy of the word and of prayer together.

11. Two important WCC world gatherings are now in view: the world mission conference at Salvador, Brazil, in 1996 and the eighth assembly at Harare, Zimbabwe. We hope that much of what we have discovered together at Ditchingham will help local churches discover appropriate ways in their own culture in which the catholic faith may be celebrated. The special nature of these global ecumenical events lies, however, in the multiplicity of churches and traditions, languages and cultures which are gathered together. The liturgies on these occasions will, we hope, show the fruit of our discussions in fresh Latin American and African cultural forms; but we need to pursue the quest which was begun in Lima, a way for the churches of the oikoumene to break bread together on the way to the unity to which the gospel calls us.

Appendix 2: The Week of Prayer

[In response to widespread interest a plenary discussion was held at Ditchingham on the materials and observance of the Week of Prayer for Christian Unity. The following text records that discussion.]

After a short presentation on the Week of Prayer for Christian Unity (the method of preparing the material) the participants were asked to tell about their experiences with the Week of Prayer in their countries/regions.

It was emphasized that church union is closely linked with prayer and that we cannot work for unity without an intensive prayer life. Prayer for unity is a pre-condition for all ecumenical work. The Week of Prayer for Christian Unity has accomplished a great deal.

> From India we were told that the material is translated into regional languages, and that the Week is very popular. It is even indicated in the newspapers.
> In the USA less attention seemed to be given to the Week of Prayer during the last years. The same is the case in Canada, where the material has a wide circulation.

In Sweden the material is used a lot.
In Ghana the material is adapted by a committee. On the local level there exists a deep commitment to and interest in ecumenism.
In Nigeria the process of adaptation normally works very well.

Suggestions

During the discussion the following suggestions were made and it became obvious that they were of general interest:

• *The date of the Week*
— In several regions the date of the Week of Prayer seems to be a problem. January is a busy time for pastors (for example Sweden and Nigeria). There could be more flexibility. Lent was mentioned as a good date with a strong symbolic meaning in context of the questions of the relationship of the different churches.
— In this context it was also mentioned that the prayer for unity in normal Sunday services should be encouraged.

• *The material for the Week*
— The themes should be chosen more carefully in terms of their international importance and acceptance.
— It was proposed to have more flexibility ("more space for their own ideas") in the liturgical material that is prepared. That would encourage pastors really to adapt the material to their local situation.

• *The wider observance of the Week*
— An effort should be made to re-establish the Week of Prayer in Eastern Europe.
— The comment was made that the Week of Prayer is "North Atlantic" in its form. The preparation group should involve people from all continents.

• *The celebration of the Week*
— The proposal was made to encourage prayer meetings in houses and families and in combination with the Bible-day observances held in some countries.
— A candle for unity could be lit on a special day of the week and in general we could find and use more symbols for unity. The printing of bookmarks indicating the Week of Prayer could be proposed to the national councils.
— Better mutual information on special events in the different churches should be encouraged which would be introduced in the intercessions. That could help us to become more aware of our belonging together. A short report about countries in special need could be added to the material.

The plenary suggested to send the adapted and translated material from the different regions/countries to the secretariat of Faith and Order. This would help the staff to get an overview of the celebration of the Week of Prayer around the world.

NOTES

[1] See "The Unity of the Church as Koinonia: Gift and Calling", 2.1, in *On the Way to Fuller Koinonia: Santiago de Compostela 1993*, eds Thomas F. Best & Günther Gassmann, Faith and Order Paper no. 166, Geneva, WCC Publications, 1994, pp.269-70.
[2] *Ibid.*, 1.1, p.269.
[3] *Ibid.*

[4] See "Koinonia in Scripture: Survey of Biblical Texts", by John Reumann, in *On the Way to Fuller Koinonia*, *op. cit.*, pp.37-69.

[5] Report of the section on unity, 1, in *The New Delhi Report: The Third Assembly of the World Council of churches, 1961*, ed. W.A. Visser 't Hooft, London, SCM, 1962, p.116.

[6] Report of section II on "What Unity Requires", 3, *Breaking Barriers: Nairobi 1975*, ed. David M. Paton, London and Grand Rapids, SPCK and Wm B. Eerdmans, 1976, p.60.

[7] Faith and Order Paper no. 111, Geneva, WCC, 1982.

[8] *Ibid.*, Baptism, 16.

[9] "Report of the General Secretary", in *Signs of the Spirit: Official Report, Seventh Assembly*, ed. Michael Kinnamon, Geneva and Grand Rapids, WCC Publications and Wm B. Eerdmans, 1991, p.167.

[10] Geneva, WCC, Unit I — Worship and Spirituality, 1994, p.11.

[11] *Ibid.*, p.19.

[12] Section III report on "Sharing a Common Life in Christ", 17, in *On the Way to Fuller Koinonia*, *op. cit.*, p.248.

[13] Report of section IV on "Worship and the Oneness of Christ's Church", 106, in *The Fourth World Conference on Faith and Order: The Report from Montreal 1963*, eds P.C. Rodger & L. Vischer, Faith and Order Paper no. 42, London, SCM, 1964, p.69.

[14] *Worship Book: Fifth World Conference on Faith and Order, Santiago de Compostela 1993*, Geneva, Commission on Faith and Order, 1993, p.vii; see *The Fourth World Conference on Faith and Order*, *op. cit.*, pp.69-80.

[15] I:I.10.

[16] II.6.

[17] "Towards Koinonia in Faith, Life and Witness: A Discussion Paper", section on "Sharing a Common Life in Christ", 76, in *On the Way to Fuller Koinonia*, *op. cit.*, p.269.

[18] *Ibid.*

[19] *With All God's People: The New Ecumenical Prayer Cycle*, compiled by John Carden, Geneva, WCC Publications, 1989.

[20] See for example *The Revised Common Lectionary*, The Consultation on Common Texts, Norwich, Canterbury Press, 1992, and *Praying Together*, English Language Liturgical Consultation, Nashville, Abingdon Press, 1988.

[21] "Some Experiences of Orthodoxy in the Search for 'Koinonia'", by Sophie Deicha, see p.81 below.

[22] "By-Laws of the Faith and Order Commission", 2, in *On the Way to Fuller Koinonia*, *op. cit.*, p.309, emphasis added.

[23] *Ibid.*, 2.c.

[24] *Ibid.*, 2.a, emphasis added.

[25] 2.1, in *On the Way to Fuller Koinonia*, *op. cit.*, p.269, emphasis added.

[26] Report of section IV on "Called to Common Witness for a Renewed World", 40, in *On the Way to Fuller Koinonia*, *op. cit.*, p.262.

[27] Report of committee II on "Worship Today", 5, in *Faith and Order, Louvain 1971: Study Reports and Documents*, Faith and Order Paper no. 59, Geneva, WCC, 1971, p.218, emphasis added.

[28] See "Information: Faith and Order", March 1994, pp.1-3; also in *Minutes of the Meeting of the Faith and Order Standing Commission*, Faith and Order Paper no. 167, Geneva, Commission on Faith and Order, 1994, pp.95-100.

[29] See "The Church as Communion: A Presentation on the World Conference Theme", by Metropolitan John of Pergamon, in *On the Way to Fuller Koinonia*, *op. cit.*, p.108.

[30] *The Third World Conference on Faith and Order held at Lund, August 15th to 28th, 1952*, ed. O.S. Tomkins, London, SCM, 1953, p.16.

[31] 1.3, in *On the Way to Fuller Koinonia*, *op. cit.*, p.269.

[32] Daily worship, Ditchingham, 22 August 1994; cf. daily worship, Santiago de Compostela, 9 August 1993, in *Worship Book: Fifth World Conference on Faith and Order*, *op. cit.*, p.12.

[33] Appendix to *Ecumenical Perspectives on Baptism, Eucharist and Ministry*, ed. Max Thurian, Faith and Order Paper no. 116, Geneva, WCC, 1983, pp. 225-46; also published in booklet form: *The Eucharistic Liturgy: Liturgical Expression of Convergence in Faith Achieved in Baptism, Eucharist and Ministry*, Geneva, WCC, 1983.

[34] See *Ecumenical Perspectives on Baptism, Eucharist and Ministry*, *op. cit.*, pp.225-36, and *The Eucharistic Liturgy*, *op. cit.*, pp.3-14.

[35] See Janet Crawford & Thomas F. Best, "Praise the Lord with the Lyre... and the Gamelan? Towards Koinonia in Worship", in *The Ecumenical Review*, vol. 46, no. 1, January 1994, pp.78-96.

II

Presentations

Worship and the Search for Christian Unity

The Contribution of, and the Challenge to, Faith and Order

JANET CRAWFORD

One of the undoubted achievements of the ecumenical movement has been to bring Christians together in prayer and worship; we have moved from praying separately for Christian unity to praying *together*. This, which is taken almost for granted today, was virtually unknown only two or three generations ago. The unfamiliarity of the experience and the difficulties it then posed can be seen in the opening service of the first world conference on Faith and Order, held in 1927. The 500 or so delegates, mostly European male church leaders and theologians, who gathered in Lausanne cathedral on that historic occasion sang two hymns, joined in silent prayer, and said the Lord's prayer and the Apostles' Creed together but in their various languages. Today, after more than sixty years, common worship is increasingly the experience of Christians not just at special ecumenical gatherings but in local churches and congregations.

Let me illustrate from my own experience. At the beginning of our academic year I attended a service held for faculty and students of the ecumenical consortium of theological colleges in which I work. The service was arranged and led by members of the Baptist college while the homily was preached by a priest from the Roman Catholic seminary. At my own college, a joint Anglican-Methodist institution, Presbyterians, Anglicans and Methodists may all preside at our community eucharist and each year we all join together in the Methodist covenant service. The music of our worship comes from two ecumenical hymn books, one Australian and one from New Zealand, from Taizé, from the Vancouver and Canberra assemblies of the WCC and from charismatic churches. On Good Friday evening I attended a Roman Catholic Church where people from all the local churches had gathered for a service of prayer, scripture and song based on Taizé worship. After Easter I attended a baptism. The child of an Anglican ordinand was baptized in an Anglican-Methodist cooperating parish by a Methodist presbyter. None of these experiences is unusual — but not one of them would have been possible in my youth.

The ecumenical movement has touched and changed the worship life of our churches and, at the local level, worship both expresses and contributes to the movement towards Christian unity. One of the tasks for our meeting is to learn more about the role of worship in the search for Christian unity at the local level, in local parishes and congregations, in united and uniting churches and in councils of churches. What has changed over recent years? What new developments are planned or looked for? How are the doctrinal convergences worked out in bilateral dialogues and in *Baptism, Eucharist and Ministry* being expressed in worship? Where are the growing points and the sticking points in common worship?

Within the World Council of Churches worship has been associated with the search for Christian unity in two ways: the practice or experience of worship, and the study of worship. It is the experience of worship which has become increasingly important, while the study of worship and theological reflection on the experience have for some time disappeared from the WCC agenda. This was perhaps to be expected, for doxology has historically come before theology. But one of the impulses for this meeting is the recognition that the time has come to recommence the study of the relationship between worship and the search for Christian unity. How does worship express the degree of koinonia/unity which we already experience? How does the experience of worship develop koinonia/unity? When and how does worship unite Christians? When and how does it divide them? How might worship facilitate or nurture the search for fuller koinonia/unity? What steps must be taken for the visible unity of the churches to be expressed in worship? These are questions which will underlie all our discussions this week.

One aspect of worship on which reflection has already begun is that of worship at ecumenical meetings (see the articles by Crawford and Best, Harling and Williams in the background documentation[1]). This type of ecumenical worship has developed greatly and there is both a quantitative and qualitative difference between the worship at the first world conference on Faith and Order in 1927 and at the fifth world conference in Santiago de Compostela in 1993, and between worship at the first WCC assembly in Amsterdam in 1948 and at the seventh assembly at Canberra in 1991. In fact the *pattern* of worship at ecumenical meetings within WCC circles has changed surprisingly little over the years. There are still usually specially prepared large opening and closing services, and a regular daily offering of morning and evening prayer, together with some opportunities for worship according to particular confessional traditions. What is different is the time and effort spent in planning and preparing worship, and the expectation of participants that worship will be a significant part of the programme. For the Faith and Order world conference at Santiago de Compostela — a relatively small world-level ecumenical meeting (though important!) — a committee met during the preceding twenty months to plan and prepare the worship and Bible studies, while at the conference itself worship was coordinated and led by a team of highly-skilled individuals from around the world.

Ecumenical worship today reflects changes brought about in the worship of the churches by such factors as the liturgical movement, the movement towards inculturation of worship, and the charismatic movement. Changes in the ecumenical movement itself are also reflected in ecumenical worship: the much greater participation of Orthodox churches and churches from Asia, Africa, Latin America and the Pacific; the greater participation of women. The much more inclusive and diverse membership of the World Council of Churches is reflected in worship that is confessionally, culturally, musically and linguistically much more diverse than in the days when the WCC was basically the preserve of European and North American Protestant churches. For many people worship at WCC assemblies and other ecumenical meetings is a highlight of their ecumenical experience, a way into the ecumenical movement at a point which engages them spiritually and emotionally. For many, ecumenical worship is a deeply-enriching experience of the worldwide nature of Christianity and of the diversity and richness of its ecclesial and cultural traditions. Such was certainly the experience of the theological students I took to the Canberra assembly in 1991. While much of the theological debate seemed to them to be abstract and irrelevant to their concerns, and while some of the politicking left them bewildered and feeling somewhat cynical, the worship engaged them in the experience of being members of a worldwide community of faith — an experience which for some of them was both life- and faith-changing. Questions which we might consider are: How can more of this rich experience be transferred and made available at the local level? How can worship in the local church make us all more conscious of the worldwide fellowship to which we belong?

We must recognize that while ecumenical worship is widely affirmed by some, it is criticized by others who would like worship to be less "ecumenical" and more "confessional". One reason for such criticism may well be because worship is

> the point at which, sometimes without recognizing it, we are most dependent on familiarity not only of liturgy and language but of style and even intonation. There is no possibility for most of us of complete freedom or unity here; and the absence of it is hard to take.[2]

Those who express this criticism seem to be mainly from the first world and I wonder if it is perhaps the cultural diversity which is the cause of discomfort. There is still however a question about the place of confessional worship at ecumenical gatherings. Related to this is the question of how we can best share the riches of our respective worship traditions and learn to appreciate those traditions different from our own. Perhaps the answer to this, which is basically a question of education, is best worked out at the local level where there are greater opportunities for mutual learning over a period of time and in the context of an actual faith-community. Another criticism of ecumenical worship which needs to be addressed is that it tends to represent the more liturgical traditions. How can the forms of worship in the more evangelical and pentecostal traditions, in the black churches and independent African churches, be more fully incorporated into ecumenical worship?

The major problem for worship at all ecumenical gatherings, the continuing point of tension, division and pain, is the celebration of the eucharist. The degree of theological convergence that has been reached still does not allow for a common celebration of the eucharist in which Orthodox, Protestants and Roman Catholics can together share communion. There is an increasing impatience with this situation, an impatience rather passionately expressed by the WCC general secretary Emilio Castro at the Canberra assembly. Referring to the main aim of the ecumenical movement as the promotion of the unity of the churches in one "eucharistic fellowship", he said:

> It is more and more frustrating that this has not been realized. We are able to be together in confronting the most divisive problems of humankind, but we are not able to heal our own history and to recognize each other within our common tradition... How can we expect to overcome divisions of life and death in the world when we are not even able to offer together the sacrifice of the Lord for the salvation of the world?... This should be the last assembly with a divided eucharist! It is not only a passionate *cri de coeur*; it is also the awareness of our real spiritual danger to prolong an ecumenism without openness to the surprises of the Spirit.[3]

This impatience is, I believe, growing at the grassroots level where particularly among the young there is an increasing disregard of ecclesiastical discipline. Might we dare to hope that at our meeting the Spirit will lead us to some new insights on this question of the eucharist?

Within the ecumenical movement the Faith and Order Commission of the World Council of Churches has the specific mandate "to proclaim the oneness of the church of Jesus Christ and to call the churches to the goal of visible unity in faith and in one eucharistic fellowship, expressed in worship and in common life in Christ, in order that the world may believe".[4] The Faith and Order movement, together with the Life and Work movement and the International Missionary Council, shaped the first phase of the ecumenical movement in the early part of this century, a phase which culminated in the formation of the World Council of Churches in 1948. The first world conference on Faith and Order (Lausanne 1927) brought together over 400 participants representing 127 Orthodox, Anglican, Reformation and free churches, in order to "register the apparent level of fundamental agreements within the conference and the grave points of disagreement remaining".[5] This comparative methodology was continued at the second world conference on Faith and Order (Edinburgh 1937). After the formation of the WCC in 1948 the tasks of the Faith and Order movement were carried on by the Faith and Order Commission within the WCC. A third world conference, held at Lund in 1952, marked the move from a comparative methodology to a form of theological dialogue which seeks to approach divisive issues from a common biblical and Christological basis. A fourth world conference was held in Montreal in 1963 and, after a long interval, the fifth world conference took place in Santiago de Compostela last year (1993). By comparison with the earlier world conferences, at Santiago de Compostela there was a much larger proportion of delegates from the southern hemisphere, more Orthodox participants, and more women. The Roman Catholic Church, a member of Faith and Order since 1968, was fully represented and there were also Evangelical and Pentecostal representatives.

Faith and Order has been justifiably called the most representative theological form in the world. The Faith and Order movement and the Faith and Order Commission have dealt with a broad spectrum of theological issues and have carried through a number of significant studies. Within the wider ecumenical movement and as part of the structure of the WCC, the Faith and Order Commission sees its task as engaging the churches in theological dialogue and common study in order to overcome the doctrinal differences which divide them. All these efforts have as their goal the manifestation of the visible unity of the church of Jesus Christ.

The first and longest-lasting involvement of Faith and Order with ecumenical prayer began in 1926 with the publication of "Suggestions for an Octave of Prayer for Christian Unity". From about 1957 a common text for the Week of Prayer for Christian Unity was prepared through informal cooperation between the Faith and Order Commission and the Roman Catholic ecumenical agency Unité chrétienne. Since 1966 the Week of Prayer for Christian Unity has been a joint project of Faith and Order and the Pontifical Council for Promoting Christian Unity (formerly the Secretariat for Promoting Christian Unity) of the Roman Catholic Church. As more occasions of common prayer have developed, this Week remains unique in that it is a time when Christians pray, together if possible, for *unity*. In some situations, the sense of urgency in this prayer has been lost. It may be that from this meeting we may make some suggestions regarding the Week of Prayer to the international preparatory group.

It was at the second world conference on Faith and Order in 1937 that for the first time the ecumenical study of worship was undertaken. Two international theological commissions were set up, one to make a comparative study of patterns of worship with a view to promoting growth in mutual understanding, and the second to study intercommunion. Both these commissions produced substantial reports which were published in 1951 under the titles *Ways of Worship* and *Intercommunion*. The study of worship was affirmed in Lund, at the third world conference on Faith and Order, where it was stated that "the work of the Commission has strengthened the conviction that worship, no less than Faith and Order, is essential to the being of the church".[6] This conviction resulted in the adding, after the world conference, of the aspect of worship to the Faith and Order mandate. The work on intercommunion influenced eucharistic worship at Lund and at future ecumenical meetings. In response to the problems caused by eucharistic worship at previous Faith and Order world conferences and the first WCC assembly, the theological commissions had recommended in relation to such worship that there be:

- a united service of preparation with emphasis on penitence for the existing state of division;
- an opportunity for all to receive communion somewhere without violation of their conscience;
- an opportunity for a general open communion, if possible on the invitation of a local church, with all invited to attend, including those unable to receive communion.

In response to a request from the WCC assembly at New Delhi in 1961 these guidelines were reviewed by the Faith and Order world conference at Montreal in 1963 and subsequently approved by the WCC central committee meeting at Rochester in 1963. These guidelines (the text is appended) have not been revised substantially since then, which surely raises the question of whether it is possible to review them and make suggestions for their revision at this meeting.

The Lund world conference also formulated what has come to be known as the Lund principle, although it was originally written as a question and a challenge. In "A Word to the Churches" agreed by the conference the following question was posed:

> Should not our churches ask themselves whether they are showing sufficient eagerness to enter into conversation with the other churches, and whether they should not act together in all matters except those in which deep differences of conviction compel them to act separately?[7]

As pointed out in the message from Santiago de Compostela the churches have made some progress in implementing this principle. But how far has it consistently and seriously been applied by the churches in their worship? What difference would it make if it were seriously applied?

At the Montreal world conference on Faith and Order in 1963 a whole section was devoted to "Worship and the Oneness of Christ's Church". Montreal emphasized the study of worship as one of the main tasks on the ecumenical agenda and also highlighted the importance of the relationship between theology and worship. However in the period after Montreal the Faith and Order Commission decided not to develop a separate study on worship, but to initiate an extended study of eucharistic theology (not eucharistic *worship*). Apart from a consultation on "Worship Today" held in Geneva in 1969 in response to a request from the Uppsala assembly of the

WCC (1968) which had struggled with the question of worship and secularization, Faith and Order has, until now, carried out no further studies on worship.

From the 1970s on, within Faith and Order interest shifted from the study of worship to detailed consideration of baptism and eucharist and the development of the convergence text, *Baptism, Eucharist and Ministry* (BEM) which received its final form at the Commission meeting in Lima, Peru, in January 1982. Discussion of the nature of worship and of the relationship between worship and the search for unity seems to have been swallowed up by the all-absorbing work on BEM, although the Commission meeting at Bangalore in 1978 did refer to the need "to grow together as a worshipping community as well as a community of faith and teaching".[8]

The Lima liturgy, intended as one possible expression of the eucharistic theology articulated in the BEM text, was prepared unofficially for use at the Lima meeting of the Commission. Since then it has been used at two WCC assemblies (Vancouver 1983 and Canberra 1991) and at many other ecumenical meetings, although it has no official status. The Faith and Order Commission has not as yet engaged in any sustained reflection or revision of what is perhaps one of its best-known products. Is this part of our task?

In conjunction with BEM, Faith and Order published in 1983 *Baptism and Eucharist: Ecumenical Convergence in Celebration*, edited by Max Thurian and Geoffrey Wainwright. With the exception of the worship resources published for the fifth world conference on Faith and Order (*Worship Book; Celebrating Community*; a prayer card) this collection of texts appears to have been the last Faith and Order publication on worship.

Following the fifth world conference in 1993, Faith and Order has entered into a new phase, a phase in which the concept of koinonia is seen as central. The major study programme planned for the next period is "The Church as Koinonia — an Ecumenical Study". It is hoped that this study will produce a short convergence document for the eighth assembly of the WCC in 1998.

This brief overview of the work of Faith and Order with regard to worship raises a number of questions for our consideration at this meeting. Some have already been mentioned: Are there suggestions to be made regarding the Week of Prayer for Christian Unity? Is it now time to review and possibly revise the Lund-Montreal-Rochester guidelines for eucharistic services at ecumenical meetings? Should we move towards a revision of the Lima liturgy? Other questions come to mind: Is it perhaps time to consider whether there should be another comparative study of worship, so that we can learn anew about our diverse traditions and see where differences and similarities now lie? And perhaps most importantly, how can the concern for worship be integrated into the ongoing work of Faith and Order and, in particular, into the ecclesiological study on "The Church as Koinonia"?

These questions and others lie before us this week and no doubt we shall only begin to address them here. At Amsterdam in 1948 the assembly said that worship is the occasion for "the showing forth of our unity, the illustration of our variety, and the confession of our situation".[9] Since then there have been many positive developments but in spite of the greater unity we experience in worship we must recognize that there is still significant division.

Let us pray that our work may contribute to the greater showing forth of our unity in and through worship. In the words of the Santiago de Compostela conference prayer:

O God, holy and eternal Trinity,
we pray for your church in all the world.
Sanctify its life; renew its worship;
empower its witness, heal its divisions;
Make visible its unity.

Appendix

Extract from *Minutes and Reports of the Seventeenth Meeting of the* [World Council of Churches] *Central Committee*, Rochester, New York, USA, 26 August-2 September 1963

B. Communion services at ecumenical gatherings

Upon the recommendation of Policy Reference Committee II, it was **agreed**:

> that the central committee, having received and noted the recommendations concerning communion services at ecumenical gatherings sent to it by the fourth world conference on Faith and Order, Montreal, adopts the recommendations embodied in the following document and transmits the document as a whole to the member churches.

1. The fourth world conference on Faith and Order noted the view of the New Delhi assembly that a reconsideration is needed of the Lund recommendations regarding "Communion Services at Ecumenical Gatherings" and agreed that this is demanded by the developments which have taken place since 1952 and the present situation within the World Council of Churches and the ecumenical movement in general.

2. There is deepened and deepening experience of unity among the churches committed to one another in the WCC. Indeed we believe that the reality, significance and implications of our *koinonia* within councils of churches in general and the WCC in particular call urgently for further study. But it should be noted that, on the one hand, there has been an increase in the number of member churches which have difficulty in accepting intercommunion between separated churches as a satisfactory concept or procedure, while on the other hand there has appeared in certain quarters and particularly among youth, though by no means confined to them, a growing impatience with certain of the traditional attitudes and hesitations on this matter. It is much to be regretted that many churches do not yet appear to have responded to the request from Lund that they give attention to differences in eucharistic theology and practice, and to the new problems in this field arising from association in the World Council of Churches. Churches owe it to themselves to relate their theologies and their disciplines to the current situation.

3. Any substantial change from the intention behind the Lund recommendations would, we believe, be widely regarded as an ecumenical disaster with widespread and unfortunate consequences. It would be a betrayal of the deepening conviction of many in the WCC, and in national and local situations, that "table fellowship" is demanded by "Christian fellowship". Moreover, whatever view is taken of intercommunion in

general, the question arises whether ecumenical gatherings do not constitute a special case. In such gatherings we have to find that arrangement of communion services which, while respecting the teaching of the churches and individual consciences, gives the fullest possible expression to the oneness of the church of Christ which we all confess.

4. Each generation must inform itself about the differences there are in eucharistic theology and practice and of the changes that are taking place. The Faith and Order Commission might well in the years ahead devote to the sacrament of holy communion the attention recently devoted to baptism. Such attention would require documentation of the eucharistic teaching and practice, including the liturgy, of the individual churches and would include careful study of recent suggestions for concelebration and an *agape*-meal. We do not feel ready to express an opinion for or against either of these. *

5. The report of the commission on intercommunion presented to the Lund conference and commended by it to the churches for their study sets forth clearly the diversity of sacramental doctrine which prevents all the churches from favouring intercommunion. We believe this report and the section on intercommunion in the report of the Lund conference are still worthy of attention. The continuing diversity of views was again stated in the report of the section on unity of the New Delhi assembly.

6. Some Christians believe that the degree of ecclesial communion which we have in the body of Christ through baptism and through our fundamental faith, although we are still divided on some points, urges us to celebrate holy communion together and to promote intercommunion between the churches. It is Christ, present in the eucharist, who invites all Christians to his table: this direct invitation of Christ cannot be thwarted by ecclesiastical discipline. In the communion at the same holy table divided Christians are committed in a decisive way to make manifest their total, visible and organic unity.

7. Some Christians believe that eucharistic communion, being an expression of acceptance of the whole Christ, implies full unity in the wholeness of his truth; that there cannot be any "intercommunion" between otherwise separated Christians; that communion in the sacraments therefore implies a pattern of doctrine and ministry, which is indivisible; and that "intercommunion" cannot presume upon the union in faith that we still seek.

8. Between these two views of holy communion there are others, some approximating to one side, some to the other. But the sharp difference of conviction indicating two poles within the Council's membership must be recognized. However, as was said at the New Delhi assembly: "For neither view can there be any final peace so long as others who are known to be in Christ are not with us at the holy communion."

9. Accordingly the central committee of the WCC agrees that the following procedure, subject to regular review, be applied to the assembly and to other WCC gatherings where it seems appropriate, and that it be recommended to the churches to their use as they may see fit. In doing so the central committee wishes to encourage the

* To assist the study by the churches of the issues involved the Faith and Order conference commended a paper on intercommunion which Frère Max Thurian is preparing (a draft of which they had seen), and the questions addressed to the churches by the consultation held at Bossey in March 1961 (*The Ecumenical Review*, vol. XIII, no. 3, April 1961).

churches, when sending delegates to conferences, to inform them of these recommendations and urge their delegates' cooperation where church discipline and individual conscience allow. It is assumed throughout that the responsibility for arranging the celebration of the sacrament rests with the churches represented at such a conference and not with the WCC itself.

It is recommended that:

a) it be made clear in the printed programme that there are at present within the fellowship of the WCC unresolved differences of eucharistic theology and practice;

b) arrangements be made within the programme of the conference for a communion service to be held at which an invitation to participate and partake is given to members of other churches; such a service should if possible be at the invitation of one of the local churches (agreed upon after consultation with such of the locally represented churches as are in membership with the WCC), or at the joint invitation of a number of such churches;

c) arrangements be made within the programme of the conference for one service of holy communion according to the liturgy of a church which cannot conscientiously offer an invitation to members of all other churches to partake of the elements; such a service should be accompanied by an invitation to all the members to be present;

d) there be in the programme a united service of preparation for holy communion at which emphasis shall be laid on (*a*) the divine mystery of salvation which the Lord's supper proclaims, (*b*) our need for Christ and his forgiveness, (*c*) sorrow for the divisions of Christendom and for their continuance, (*d*) the unity in Christ given and experienced within the World Council of Churches, and (*e*) our responsibility to pray and work for a fuller manifestation of this unity;

e) there be an opportunity outside the conference programme for communion services at such times as make it possible for every member of the conference to receive communion without violation of conscience or disloyalty to church tradition;

f) it be recognized as fitting that arrangements be made for those whose normal practice is that of frequent or daily participation in holy communion; such individuals should be invited to give special consideration to the attitude they should take to the service proposed in paragraph (b), particularly when this is held on a Sunday;

g) where a conference is held in a place where there is only one member church and this church is unable to issue an open invitation, but is willing to arrange a celebration of the liturgy at which the members of the conference are invited to be present, such a liturgy be held on the first Sunday of the conference; but the conference authorities be empowered to make place in the programme for a service at which an invitation to participate and partake is given in accordance with paragraphs (b) and (h);

h) should an assembly or other WCC gathering be held in a place where no member church is represented locally, it should be regarded as appropriate that those responsible for the programme, after careful consultation with the churches sending delegates, invite one or more of these churches to make arrangements for services of holy communion in accordance with paragraphs (b) and (c).

NOTES

[1] Janet Crawford & Thomas F. Best, "Praise the Lord with the Lyre...and the Gamelan?: Towards Koinonia in Worship", *The Ecumenical Review*, vol. 46, no. 1, January 1994, pp.78-96; "The Liturgy of the World: Ecumenical Worship with All Senses", by Per Harling, the introduction to *Worshipping Ecumenically: Orders of Service from Global Meetings with Suggestions for Local Use*, ed. Per Harling, Geneva, WCC Publications, 1995, pp.1-26; "The Goal of Visible Unity and the Limits of Diversity: (a) Visible Unity", by Rowan Williams, *Returning Pilgrims: Insights from the Fifth World Faith and Order Conference, Santiago de Compostela*, London, Council of Churches for Britain and Ireland, 1994, pp.12-13.

[2] *Breaking Barriers: Nairobi 1975*, ed. David M. Paton, London and Grand Rapids, SPCK/Eerdmans, 1975, p.8.

[3] *Signs of the Spirit: Official Report of the Seventh Assembly: Canberra, Australia, 7-20 February 1991*, ed. Michael Kinnamon, Geneva, WCC, 1991, p.167.

[4] By-laws of the Faith and Order Commission, 2, in *On the Way to Fuller Koinonia*, eds Thomas F. Best & Günther Gassmann, Geneva, WCC, 1994, p.309.

[5] From the Preamble to the reports from the conference, in *Faith and Order: Proceedings of the World Conference, Lausanne, August 3-21, 1927*, ed. H.N. Bate, London, SCM, 1927, p.459.

[6] *The Third World Conference on Faith and Order held at Lund, August 15th to 28th, 1952*, ed. O.S. Tomkins, London, SCM, 1953, p.39.

[7] *Ibid.*, p.16.

[8] *Sharing in One Hope: Commission on Faith and Order Bangalore 1978, Reports and Documents*, Faith and Order Paper no. 92, Geneva, WCC, 1978, p.249.

[9] *The First Assembly of the World Council of Churches*, ed. W.A. Visser 't Hooft, London, SCM, 1949, p.28.

Knowing Something a Little

On the Role of the *Lex Orandi* in the Search for Christian Unity

GORDON LATHROP

Among the Dene peoples of northern Canada there is one people, commonly called the Yellowknife, who have known themselves as the *Tetsot'ine*, "those who know something a little".[1] Their name reflects the respectful and careful common life of a people surrounded by a vast and mysterious land marked by powerful natural forces: no one knows everything about such a land. But their name also reflects a community that treasures the life-giving, survival-enabling skills of the things they do know together. Of course, their name is a gentle rebuke to the usual attitude of dominant cultures. Borrowed as the title for these reflections, such a name may stand as an invitation to us, at the outset of a conversation about worship and ecumenism, to enter into our work with both humility and truth — to know the things we do really know, especially those things without which we cannot survive as Christians, and to be silent before the great mysteries which remain.

We do indeed know something. This gathering knows prayer, even common prayer. It knows that many Christians have been finding each other again in common prayer. We know the "holy things" which are set out for the "holy people" in the assemblies of Christ's church, and we know the One who, in the midst of these things and this people, is the Only Holy. We do not thereby understand all the mysteries of the unity or of the disunity of Christ's church. But we do know something a little.

Prosper's method and ours

Let us begin with what we know.

That is, of course, what Prosper of Aquitaine (ca. 390-463) was doing when he wrote that classic argument for the necessity and availability of grace for all people which has come to be summarized in the phrase *lex orandi, lex credendi*, "the rule for prayer is the rule for belief". What Prosper actually wrote was this:

> Let us also look at the sacred witness of the public priestly prayers which, handed down by the apostles, are celebrated in the same way in all the world and in every catholic church, so that the rule of praying should establish the rule of believing (*ut legem credendi lex statuat supplicandi*). For when the leaders of the holy peoples perform the mission entrusted to them, they plead the cause of humankind before the divine clemency, and, sustained by the sighs of the whole church, they implore and pray that faith may be given to the unbelieving, that idolaters may be liberated from the errors of their impiety...[2]

So, here is *something*: all the churches, all the assemblies of the holy people, regularly — every Sunday, every day — intercede with God for everyone, even their enemies, following the explicit counsel of 2 Timothy 2:1-4[3] and the universal historical practice of Christian gatherings. Knowing this profoundly Christian "something", knowing it even a little, supports and establishes this article of catholic faith: that everyone needs God and God's grace, that grace is, a priori, not denied to anyone, and that faith does not come about without grace.

In making such an argument, Prosper was only articulating in a new situation what had been done before him in other situations — in response to the challenges of Gnosticism, Arianism or Pelagianism, for example — by many other theologians and teachers of the church. Augustine, Ambrose, Cyril of Jerusalem, John Chrysostom, Irenaeus, Ignatius — each one turned either to baptismal practice or to the fact of real bread and wine used in the eucharist or to the participatory character of the gathering around the eucharistic table to support, even to *discover* his arguments. The experienced worship practice of the church counted in the church's theological discussion. Teachers needed to pay attention to worship. As Evagrius of Pontus had said: "If you are a theologian, you will pray in truth; if you pray in truth, you will be a theologian."[4]

But it was not just *any* practice, not whatever one might encounter being done in a supposedly Christian assembly, which was the source for establishing the faith of the church.[5] For Prosper, the *lex supplicandi* which established the *lex credendi* was a practice which had biblical grounding, universal acceptance, actual local congregational exercise, and some accompanying sense that it had God's approval.[6] And it was a *practice*, a thing that was done. The mere fact that it was done — not so much the specific text of its liturgical realization — was the ground for the theological assertion which followed.[7]

Can we follow Prosper's method? Of course, we will recognize that *lex credendi* also influences *lex orandi*. The teaching of bishops and theologians, especially as that teaching has been reflection on the meaning of the language of faith alive in the church, has had a critical role in the reformation of worship. The point is not to argue against the importance of either theology or *magisterium* here. Furthermore, we will know that diversity in the practice of the churches is not necessarily wrong nor necessarily destructive of unity. It can be a sign of fidelity and a gift of mutual enrichment that the gospel of Jesus Christ is celebrated in different places in different ways. But can we ask what practices among us give an experience basis for communion between these different Christian assemblies? And can we ask, with Prosper, whether these practices have biblical grounding, universal acceptance, actual local congregational exercise, and some sense of God's approval? Can we, together, know something a little?

Ecumenical experience

In fact, recent experiences in the life of the churches have been full of such growing knowledge. The Constitution on the Sacred Liturgy of the Second Vatican Council enunciated principles which the movements for liturgical renewal have been bringing alive in the worship assemblies of many churches: active participation of all the faithful, clarity and strength of both word and sacrament, "church" as primarily liturgical assembly, leadership as service to the assembly. Indeed, "word and sacrament" as a brief description of the centre of Christian assembly shows up in Methodist, Anglican, Roman Catholic, Presbyterian, Lutheran circles and in many other places.

Evidence of this does not reside only in documents. Many of us have been going to church and finding a new clarity of "word and sacrament" in our churches. That is, we have been finding a new accent on the importance of scripture reading in harmony with other Christians using a common lectionary, a new sense of the importance of doing baptisms in the midst of the Christian community as it is gathered, and a continued and steady growth in the frequency of the celebration or reception of the holy supper.

Furthermore, the *Baptism, Eucharist and Ministry* document has helped churches to see not simply the possibility of shared *meanings* in the sacraments but the presence of shared *patterns* in their celebration, in the actual, local facts of their observance. Theologians now not uncommonly end their writings with suggestions for celebration which they presume can be ecumenically received since the ecumenical patterns have begun so closely to approximate each other. The availability of Roman Catholic worship in the vernacular for almost three decades has meant that many non-Roman Christians have experienced the shock of familiarity when they have visited local Roman Catholic worship — and vice versa. And the various liturgical resources produced for diverse churches throughout the world in the same three decades — resources which depend on the same liturgical historical scholarship and the same Christian assessments of the need of the present time[8] — look remarkably alike in basic structure and remarkably alike in the conviction to put that basic structure into forms that are responsive to the diverse local cultures.

Even some churches which might have originally thought that the sources of liturgical scholarship or of the "Lima document" were too "high church" or too narrowly sacramental have found themselves immersed in a renewed accent on the practice and meaning of baptism and the Lord's supper. In the United States and Canada, vigorous "evangelical churches" have become interested in what they call "convergence worship", making use of the fruits of the twentieth-century liturgical movement while, at the same time, inviting the classic "liturgical churches" to see their own evangelical callings more clearly.[9] The Quakers and others, whose refusals of otherwise nearly universal worship practices can be regarded as "critical" or even "catholic exceptions",[10] have taken up their calling, not of rejecting catholic worship practice but of inviting us all to interpret the practice more deeply and widely: baptism is the participation in the Spirit-led community; the word must inform all of our life; every meal is, in some sense, the Lord's supper. For this insight the Friends need the Catholic practice, but the Catholics also need the Friends.

Such a survey is not exhaustive. It only begins to suggest what we have been coming to know together a little. What has been missing is serious ecumenical thought that proceeds from this growing common knowledge. Here, now, we can establish a little more clearly the central characteristics of the shared rule of prayer, and we can sketch something of the implications which flow from this rule of prayer for the rule of faith in our own present situation of need.

Ordo* as *lex orandi

What is the *lex orandi*? What things in the worship of the churches have biblical grounding, universal acceptance, local exercise and the widespread trust that they are under God's approval? One way to articulate an answer is this: common to the different churches is the deepest structure of the *ordo* of Christian worship, the received and universal pattern or shape and scheduling of Christian liturgy.[11] This *ordo* organizes *a participating community together with its ministers gathered in song and prayer around the scriptures read and preached, around the baptismal washing, enacted or remembered, and around the holy supper*. The *ordo* is these things done together, side by side.

By this view, the ecumenical rule of prayer is the teaching and the washing which constitute baptism in all of our churches. It is the gathering, reading of scripture and preaching, interceding, setting out of bread and wine together with *eucharistia*, eating and drinking, and collecting for the poor which increasingly constitute the central Sunday assembly in most of our churches. Note: the *ordo* is scripture reading together with preaching, eucharistia together with eating and drinking. It is ministers together with people, choir together with congregation, thanksgiving together with beseeching. It is also the psalms and prayers of the week together with the Sunday assembly, the observances of the year together with the annual *pascha*. And it is all of this done so that in the power of the Spirit people may be gathered into the grace of Jesus Christ to stand before and bear witness to the love of God.

But does this, this way of stating the rule of prayer in the churches, meet Prosper's criteria? We might spend time here discussing the actual current universality of such an *ordo*, the role and meaning of the "critical exceptions" to its universality, and the extent to which it is a lively goal for renewal in the churches. We might also discuss the extent to which this *ordo* currently has the confidence of Christian believers as being under God's blessing.[12] But the practices this *ordo* describes are, indeed, local and congregational, and, to the extent we are able to know actual worship history, these very practices can be seen to be the leading characteristics of most catholic churches throughout the twenty centuries of Christianity. In any case, it needs to be noted that the rule of prayer is determined not simply by biblical texts nor by historical incidence nor by statistical surveys of universality, but by all of these things working together in the living experience of the church and encouraging us towards renewal.

Biblical foundation and meaning

But, to begin with the foundation, is this *ordo* indeed biblical or, to say it with Prosper, is it "apostolic"? Can we discuss its biblical grounding? Yes. In fact, we begin to come close to the deeper reasons for its centrality — the actual survival reasons for this "something" we know a little, the force of this rule of prayer for establishing the rule of faith — when we look at the New Testament. For the sake of understanding the reasons for the rule of prayer, let us look more closely at the biblical grounding of its leading characteristics: baptism, word and eucharist.

These core actions of the current churches are also found in the biblical record. To the extent that it is possible for us to ascertain, all the communities behind the New Testament writings treasure baptism, making use of it as the way one enters the church. The reading of scripture as a liturgical practice is implied by passages in Luke, where the interpretation of scripture by the risen Lord is probably a model of the church's Sunday meeting, by passages in Paul, where the apostle's own letters are to be read in the gathered assembly, and by the letters to the churches and the opening of the scroll in the Revelation to John.[13] Preaching — like the risen Lord's interpretation of scripture on the first day of the week — is everywhere assumed. Furthermore, the Christian practice of the supper of the Lord is assumed by the "do this" of Luke and Paul[14] and by diverse reports elsewhere in the New Testament. For example, that the meal is held every Sunday is reported for the community at Troas and suggested by the first-day model of the Emmaus story: the risen Lord interprets the scripture and is known in the blessing and sharing of the bread.[15]

There are even passages which hold more than one of these core actions together. At the beginning of Acts, after the baptism of a great multitude of new believers, the community is "devoted... to the apostles' teaching and fellowship, to the breaking of bread and the prayers" (2:42). At Troas, the community gathers on Sunday for preaching and the meal (20:7-12), the same pattern which is found in the disciples' first-day meeting with the risen One on the way to Emmaus (Luke 24:13-22). In Mark, Jesus uses together the cup and baptism, central matters which the community knows, as metaphors for the martyrs' death (Mark 10:38-39). Paul depends upon the community having baptism and the meal as central events in order to make his exhortation based on the "baptism" of Israel in the Red Sea and the holy eating and drinking of the exodus journey (1 Cor. 12:13).

None of these passages gives us great ritual detail about what the churches did when they gathered for worship. But this much is clear: in New Testament texts, the risen Christ bids the community to teach and to baptize (Matt. 28:19; cf. Mark 16:16), the crucified risen One is known in the explanation of scripture and in the meal (Luke 24:30-32; cf. John 20:20; Rev. 5:6-7), and preaching is full of the powerful weakness of the cross of Christ (1 Cor. 1:17). These assertions of Christian faith only serve to underline the crucial significance of these central symbolic acts already among New Testament era communities.

But these assertions also do more. They help us to see the deepest reason why the actions of "the core" are the core: because they have to do with Jesus Christ. More: because in them we are enabled to encounter the full reality of who Jesus is and what he does, and so we are brought to stand before God in the power of the Spirit as one body in Christ. The core actions are not so much commanded by scripture nor dependent upon a certain view of biblical theology. They are rather matters which have lived on in the churches, matters which those churches have seen as "apostolic". They are the means by which the current churches are in communion with those ancient assemblies. When New Testament churches present one of these things as done by dominical command, they present the central matters of their actual practice, matters they saw as having to do with the crucified-risen One, matters in which we are in communion with them. There are certainly other things which some Christian communities did when they worshipped: ecstatic utterance, for example, or singing. But these things — baptism, preaching, the supper — came to be especially central to Christians because they have been seen as intimately bound up with who Christ is.

We see this connection of Jesus with those things that become the church's central actions already in the gospel traditions of his life. According to the gospels, Jesus himself was *baptized*.[16] He himself came *preaching*.[17] And one of the ways he was most well-known — even notorious — was by his constant *table-fellowship* with sinners.[18] By this perspective, the church's gatherings around these very things simply continue the actions of Jesus himself.

But we see the connection of Jesus Christ to the core actions of the church's worship even more strongly in the ongoing tradition of faith that participation in these things is participation in him. To be part of the community of preaching, baptism and the meal is to be gathered, by the power of the Spirit, "into him", so to stand in him under the grace of the very God who sent him. Thus, in the New Testament, Jesus Christ is the meaning of the scriptures and the content of preaching;[19] speaking of him is speaking the "yes" to all of God's ancient scriptural promises.[20] Baptism is being buried with Christ in order to be raised to newness of life with him, and this resurrection occurs "by the glory of the Father".[21] And Jesus Christ hosts the supper and is himself the very gift given for eating and drinking;[22] to eat and drink with him is to be formed as his body[23] and to stand with him as he blesses and gives thanks to God.

The New Testament does not give us a constitution of the church nor a service book. It does give us Jesus Christ, seen and known amid ordinary things — water for washing, words for telling important stories and for prayer, a shared meal. Just as access to Christ would be difficult and skewed for us without the New Testament books, so also we need the concrete signs of water, communal words and shared meal. Without them, when we speak of Jesus Christ we could easily be speaking more of ourselves and of our own projections than of the biblical, historic Christ. It is very easy to take a holy figure — "Jesus" — and make that figure a screen on which we show our own ideas or needs. But with these concrete things, we encounter the very *self* of Jesus breaking into our projected ideas:[24] in the teaching, baptizing church, "I am with you always" (Matt. 28:20); the scriptures themselves "testify of me" (John 5:39); in the meal, "this is my body" (Mark 14:22). These things are central to us, because Christ is central to us. These things are to us as the very flesh of Christ, the concrete way of our encounter with him who is for us the revelation and the gift of the fullness of God's grace.

Lex orandi, lex credendi

Several important consequences follow from this deepest, "apostolic" reason for the core actions of Christian worship. When we begin to trace those consequences we begin to see the implications of this rule of prayer for the rule of faith. For one thing, it is clear that we *need* this core, these central symbols. These things we know have to do with our survival. As the deacon Emeritus and his companions said, in the midst of the persecutions of Diocletian (284-305), when they were accused of participating in the Sunday assembly: "We cannot *be* without the *dominicum*."[25] Now, in the late twentieth century, there are a lot of people who are talking about Jesus Christ. That name is used for many religious ideas present in our current cultures — for success programmes and for self-realization plans, for politics of the left and of the right, for various requirements for what human beings must be, for ideas about the "soul" and about world-escape. Indeed, some people use the name "Jesus" as if it were a perfect synonym for popular religion or, simply, for one's own self. Other, more scholarly sorts, assume that the only access to Jesus is through reconstructions of what he might have actually been like, what he might have actually said, reconstructions which are similarly, though more subtly, prey to the same pressures of current politics and religion, now operative in the "reconstructor". Other peoples in the world still need to hear of Jesus Christ for the first time. The Christian church has classically believed that who Jesus is and what he does are most reliably encountered in "word and sacrament", that is in the scriptures read next to that bath and that meal which are full of Jesus' own, self-giving "I".

In Christ in the communion of the Spirit, according to Christian faith, we meet the God who wipes away tears, gives life to the dead, promises and says "yes" to the promises, and sets out the food of forgiveness and festival. We, then, need Christ, the historic biblical Christ, and not simply our own projections and ideas of him. By this view, "church" is none other than the assembly which does these things in which we encounter Christ, in which the Spirit acts. Many other ideas of the meaning of "church" abound in ecumenical discussion. This is the view which arises from the rule of prayer.

But why *these things*, specifically? Why this *ordo*, this rule of prayer? Why not something else? Why not some other book or some other religious rites? Conch-shell blowing or incense-burning or pilgrimages, for example? There is nothing wrong with such rites per se; in fact some Christians make use of them in their own communities, as accessory to the central things. Furthermore, there are many other beautiful and profound books besides the Bible. But the stories of Israel set next to the ancient books from the earliest church are found by the church as the way to encounter Jesus Christ. The washing which is baptism and the supper which is "eucharist" were already present in his life, as witnessed in the gospels. Indeed, scripture reading and interpretation, washing and purity before God and prayers at meals or the meal-as-prayer were deeply present in the lay religious/Jewish culture in which Jesus' ministry first occurred. According to the New Testament, he made use of them for the purposes of his own mission. Then, these things were received, down through the ages, as gifts from him, done at his command. We might speculate about other possibilities. But we actually have no other means. These are the ones which are historically present in the New Testament and are found nearly universally in the life of the church. These concrete, real things connect us to a concrete, real history of the church.

And they connect us to the concrete, real earth. While we may say that we have these things simply because they are what actually comes to us from the culture in which Jesus was born and from the history of the church, Christian faith has believed that the universal availability of the stuff of these central symbols has been a gift from God. Water is everywhere. Humans need it simply to live. Baptism is in water, any water, not some special or Near-Eastern water. Accessible but strongly symbolic speech, used to convey the deepest human values, is found in every culture. But then the oral witness to Jesus Christ can be made in that language and the Bible can be translated into it. Festive meals are found universally. The Lord's supper is held with local bread and local wine — or, where these are simply not available or are far too expensive, with locally recognized staple food and festive drink — not with special, imported food. But then the things in which we encounter Jesus Christ and, in him, God's overflowing grace for all, are accessible everywhere and are easily seen to be signs of the goodness of God's earth, as well as signs for the deep unity which God's mercy can establish between the good diversity of the many cultures of the world.

Furthermore, "word", "bath" and "meal" can be seen to be gifts which are inclusive in another sense. Words can be both praise and lament, the recounting of both death and life. Both are used in the stories of Israel and of Jesus and both are welcome in the church. A bath can wash and a bath can drown. Both happen in the one use of water in the church. The joyful, life-giving meal of the community has the death of Jesus at the centre of its memory and the dreadful hunger of our neighbours and of the world as the focus of our resultant mission. The central things of Christian worship are not narrowly "religious" things nor are they concerned only with happiness and success. They welcome us, who gather to do them, to the full truth about ourselves: sorrow and hope, hunger and food, loneliness and community, sin and forgiveness, death and life. God in Christ comes amidst these things, full of mercy.

That these historic, central matters of Christian worship correspond to *mercy* can be seen in the simplest encounter with their forms. Words may be *heard*, coming from outside of ourselves, giving us a new story or reinserting us in an old story, whereby we may understand ourselves and our world anew. Water may be *poured* over us, somebody else thereby immersing us in the bath. Food may be *given* to us — and to lines and lines of other people — pressed into our hands, reached to our lips. These communal gifts, in their very form, show forth and enact the Christian faith that God's grace in Christ is our new story, our bath, our life-giving meal.

But why *all* of these things? Would not just one be enough? No. The gift is more abundant than that. A set of words alone could easily be twisted into a new law, a list of things we have to do in order to be acceptable to God, unless it is constantly clear that the content of the words is the same content which is washed over us in the bath and given to us to eat and drink in the supper. Drinking the cup in which Christ says "my blood, for you" gives us a key to understand the scriptures. All preachers should strive to see that their sermons say in words the same thing that the bath and the cup say in actions. In the church, words should be edible, like bread, and just as full of grace. And the bread of Christ is to be seen as a "word", indeed one of the strongest words we have to say the truth about God, the world and ourselves. This is why, in the history of the Christian liturgy, the essential matters are always juxtaposed to each other and are always themselves made up of at least two juxtaposed elements: readings *and* preaching, teaching *and* bathing, thanksgiving *and* receiving the food.[26] The Christian *ordo* is the simple pattern that results when these basic things are done side-by-side.

Ecumenical implications

It then becomes clear that Christian worship has a responsibility to let these things always *be* and *be seen to be* at the centre of our gatherings. The word "worship" itself may mislead us into thinking that when we gather we may do anything which seems appropriate to us as "worship" — any sort of singing, any sort of "god-talk", any sort of exercise in a stained-glass-windowed hall. But if our gathering is about the grace of God in Jesus Christ and if the communion between our gatherings is to be based on the confession of that grace,we cannot do without "word and sacrament". To pretend that "Christian freedom" includes freedom from these things may be only to choose the bondage of our own opinions, our own "religion", our own, unrelieved selves, masquerading as "God".

At the same time, that these things are essential to Christian worship should not be seen as a burden. They are gifts. They should be celebrated as gifts. Indeed, there can be great diversity in the ways in which an assembly reads scripture and interprets it, washes those joining the community and holds a meal. There can be many other secondary characteristics — musical style, architectural or artistic arrangement, patterns of entrance and leaving, leadership — which may make one assembly observing the central things seem very different from another. Yet these assemblies, sharing the rule of prayer, will recognize and encourage each other.

From these reflections on the *lex orandi* there follow at least five concrete implications for ecumenism and for the *lex credendi* today:

1. For *inculturation:* Worship is not and ought not be the same everywhere. Indeed, the unity we seek will always be a communion between local churches. The rule of prayer helps us to see that local churches are none other than the communities which do the word and sacraments. But these communities must enact these central things *locally*: in language and gesture, ritual and song which is locally accessible,

unfolding local gifts. They are always the catholic church dwelling in *this particular place*. But they are also *the catholic church* dwelling here. The universal gift of word and sacrament give to them something to inculturate, a pattern into which to draw the deepest local gifts.[27]

2. For *communion:* the *ordo* of Christian worship, the deep pattern we share, is a major means of the communion between these local churches, a principal part of the *koina* which enable *koinonia*. This deep pattern, however, should not only be used as a tool for *recognition*, helping us to see that the other church is indeed truly Christian, but also as a means for mutual encouragement to renewal. As Prosper's argument should encourage all catholic churches continually to recover priestly intercession for the world, so the whole rule of prayer can be the subject of mutual ecumenical recommendation. "Are scriptures and preaching, *eucharistia* and eating and drinking, teaching and washing clear and central in your assemblies?" we may ask each other. In fact, such inquiries may need now to be the first agenda item of an ecumenical movement newly interested in the communion of local churches.

3. For *ecumenical theology:* In the manner pioneered by the Lima document, work should continue to re-situate many of the classic disagreements between Christians within the context of the rule of prayer, of the "something we know a little". Much clarity is obtained when baptismal conflicts are placed within the full *ordo* of teaching and washing for the sake of communal discipleship, when ministry conflicts are made to refer to actual functions within the assembly, when debates about "sacrifice" are seen to be discussions about the meaning of eating and drinking the gift of Christ in the holy supper, and when arguments about action for social justice are rooted in the implications of the Sunday eucharist. For example, believer-baptist groups may be able to see themselves as enrolling their young children in a "catechumenate", recognizable to many other Christians, while infant-baptizing groups may find their own life-long call to discipleship refreshed, and both groups will find themselves called to a strong celebration of baptism which shows forth its centrality and meaning. We will be helped in these discussions if bishops and theologians are encouraged to reflect upon and learn from the shared worship patterns of the churches and if the voices of liturgical scholars are also welcomed to the table.

4. For *ecumenical worship:* When ecumenical worship occurs — in councils and assemblies of the churches, but also in local instances of mutual reconciliation — it will be the deep and simple pattern of the shared rule of prayer which will predominate, with an eclectic use of cultural and denominational material to illuminate and unfold that pattern. We will need to move beyond "demonstration liturgies" — showing an ecumenical gathering how one particular group does worship — if these liturgies only serve to obscure the shared pattern and make impossible a common community of prayer. A core realization of the *lex orandi* is that the actual gathering of Christians does *its* liturgy. In ecumenical gatherings that shared liturgy can only be the shared *ordo* unfolded with such instances of local song or local art as can be received as mutually enriching.

5. For *the life of the world:* But we will be most helped if we remember that the essential reason for this rule of prayer is that the church might speak and sign the mercy of God in Jesus Christ for the sake of the life of the world. Word, table, bath occur at the heart of a participating community so that all people may freely encounter God's mercy in Christ, that they may come to *faith* again and again, that they may be formed into a community of faith, that they may stand in dignity, life and freedom

before God, that they may be brought to the possibility of love for God's world. When these reasons are not manifest in the exercise of the central things themselves, the deep meaning of the rule of prayer is obscured and betrayed. Even so, God acts in these things. God's life-giving Spirit breaks out of our prisons. But our purpose must be to let the reason for the rule of prayer be apparent in inculturation, be the goal for the urgency of ecumenical *koinonia* and ecumenical theology, and be the theme of ecumenical prayer. The rule of prayer shows a pattern of reading together with preaching which leads to intercessions for the world, of thanksgiving together with eating and drinking which leads to collection for the poor and mission in the world. In fact, all the pairs of the *lex orandi* are understood most clearly when they are understood as yielding such a witness to God's universal mercy. For Prosper and for us, that is the *lex credendi* which the rule of prayer always establishes.

Grace alive in word and sacrament: that is the "something" we know a little, around which this meeting may gather, to which we may continually recall each other.

Near this place, there was, in the fourteenth century, a woman whose steady life in the sacrament and in the word, reached into her anchorite's cell from the community's assembly-room, yielded such a vision of God's mercy:

> I saw that for us he is everything that is good, comforting and helpful; he is our clothing, who, for love, wraps us up, holds us close; he entirely encloses us for tender love, so that he may never leave us... And in this fashion all things have their being by the grace of God.[28]

May our encounter here with the rule of prayer, with the something we know a little, with the central matters for Christian survival in a continually mysterious world, yield just such a vision renewed within us. May our liturgies proclaim with renewed force that in Christ God holds all the world in tender love.

NOTES

[1] For a moving fictional account of the first encounters between the *Tetsot'ine* and Europeans in the nineteenth century see Rudy Wiege, *A Discovery of Strangers*, Toronto, Knopf, 1994.

[2] "Obsecrationum quoque sacerdotalium sacramenta respiciamus, quae ab apostolis tradita in toto mundo atque in omni ecclesia catholica uniformiter celebrantur, ut legem credendi lex statuat supplicandi. Cum enim sanctarum plebium praesules mandata sibimet legatione fungantur, apud divinam clementiam humani generis agunt causam et, tota secum ecclesia congemiscente, postulant et precantur ut infidelibus donetur fides, ut idololatrae ab impietatis suae liberentur erroribus..." PL 51:209-210; cf. P. DeClerck, *La "prière universelle" dans les liturgies latines anciennes*, Münster, Aschendorff, 1977, p.89; and G. Wainwright, *Doxology*, New York, Oxford, 1980, pp.225-26.

[3] That this reference is what Prosper means by *ab apostolis tradita* is made clear by other writings; see especially PL 51:664-665.

[4] PG 79:1180b.

[5] For example, one recent collection demonstrates a variety of ancient Christian ritual practices — popular and even communal practices — which have not been regarded as source for the "rule of faith". See Marvin Meyer & Richard Smith, *Ancient Christian Magic: Coptic Texts of Ritual Power*, San Francisco, Harper, 1994.

[6] Prosper continues: "Haec autem non perfunctorie neque inaniter a Domino peti, rerum ipsarum monstrat effectus. Quandoquidem ex omni errorum genere plurimos Deus dignatur attrahere quos erutos de potestate tenebrarum transferat in regnum filii charitatis suae." PL 51:210.

[7] For two fine modern discussions of the *lex orandi* see K. Irwin, *Context and Text: Method in Liturgical Theology*, Collegeville, Liturgical Press, 1994, and Wainwright, *Doxology, op. cit.*, pp.218-250. It should be noted that the *lex orandi* was an experienced practice — what can be called *theologia prima* — together with reflection on the universality and the meaning of that practice. On *theologia prima* see Aidan Kavanagh, *On Liturgical Theology*, New York, Pueblo, 1984. On the inter-relation of *lex orandi, lex credendi* and *lex agendi* see Kevin Irwin, *Liturgical Theology: A Primer*, Collegeville, Liturgical Press, 1992.

[8] Liturgical scholars, who have shared this scholarship and these pastoral assessments, are frequently surprised when they discover theologians still struggling over issues which belong to other pastoral times and seem appropriate only to radically different forms of the liturgy than those celebrated today.

[9] See Robert E. Webber, ed., *The Complete Library of Christian Worship*, vol. 3, Nashville, Star Song, 1993, pp.122-24,196-99. For an example of "convergence" interest in Great Britain, applied to music for worship, see Andrew Wilson-Dickson, *The Story of Christian Music*, Oxford, Lion, 1992.

[10] Wainwright, *Doxology, op. cit.*, p.244; cf. Gordon Lathrop, *Holy Things: A Liturgical Theology*, Minneapolis, Fortress, 1993, pp.157-58.

[11] Since the work of Gregory Dix, much of Christian liturgical scholarship has been interested in "shape" and pattern. Alexander Schmemann, in *Introduction to Liturgical Theology*, New York, St Vladimir's Seminary, 1975, moved this reflection on pattern towards a reflection on *ordo*. The 1995 congress of the international and ecumenical Societas Liturgica will be on the theme "The Future Shape of the Liturgy". For a recent reflection on the *ordo* of the liturgy, see Lathrop, *Holy Things*. Portions of what follows have been worked out in greater detail in Gordon Lathrop, *What Are the Essentials of Christian Worship?*, Minneapolis, Augsburg, 1994.

[12] Geoffrey Wainwright's criteria for a practice to be part of the "rule of prayer" include biblical origin, universal acceptance in time and place, and holiness or ethical consequence. See *Doxology, op. cit.*, pp.242-45.

[13] Luke 24:27,32,45; cf. 4:21; 1 Thessalonians 5:27; Colossians 4:16; Revelation 2-3; 5:1-10.

[14] Luke 22:19; 1 Corinthians 11:24-25.

[15] Acts 20:7; Luke 24:30-31.

[16] Mark 1:9 and parallels.

[17] Mark 1:14 and parallels.

[18] Cf. Matthew 11:19; Luke 7:34.

[19] Luke 24:27; 1 Corinthians 1:23; Revelation 5:5.

[20] 2 Corinthians 1:20.

[21] Romans 6:4.

[22] Mark 14:23-24 and parallels; Revelation 3:20.

[23] 1 Corinthians 10:17.

[24] Cf. Edward Schillebeeckx, *Tussentijdsverhaal over twee Jezus boeken*, Bloemendaal, Nelissen, 1978, pp.31-34.

[25] "...sine dominico non possumus". See Wily Rordorf, *Sabbat und Sonntag in der Alten Kirche*, Zurich, Theologischer Verlag, 1972, p.109.

[26] See Lathrop, *Holy Things, op. cit.*, pp.204-206 and passim.

[27] Thus, Gerrit Singgih of Indonesia, in a private conversation, reports that, in Java, denominational, contextual and contemporary ways of worship can be drawn into mutual enrichment by a focus on the *sacraments*.

[28] Julian of Norwich, *Revelations of Divine Love*, trans. by M.L. del Mastro, New York, Doubleday, 1977, p.88.

Unity and Prayer

THOMAS FITZGERALD

We are gathered here today because of the prayers of others. Over the course of years, decades and centuries, Christian men and women have prayed for the unity of Christ's church. In their prayer, they have responded to the divine initiative. They have responded to the love of God the Father in Christ through the Spirit. They have prayed that divisions be healed, that those who are separated be reconciled. Throughout the ages and until our own day, all of these prayers have echoed the prayer of Our Lord, "that they may be one as the Father and I are one..." (John 17:21).

We can never know the full force of these prayers. But we can catch a glimpse of their fruits from time to time. Their fruits are to be seen where there is an increase of love, a deepening of understanding, a desire to break down walls of division, and, most importantly, a willingness to change for the sake of the gospel.

When the early Christian teachers reflected upon the realities of Christian division, it seems to me that two observations predominated.

First, divisions among Christians are rooted in a "hardness of heart". This fundamental sin is at the root of every division. It is "hardness of heart" which leads to the unwillingness to reconcile, to pride, to arrogance, and to the absence of love. St Maximos the Confessor stated the case very simply when he said: "Believe me, my children, nothing else has caused heresy and schism in the church but the fact that we do not love God and our neighbour."[1]

Second, the early teachers of the church tell us that Christian reconciliation results not simply from formal doctrinal agreement. They certainly would not diminish the value of theological discussion and the significance of credal statements. History shows us that formal statements of reconciliation are necessary and important. But these credal statements and formal agreements must be fashioned and must be received by persons whose hearts are open to the healing power of God. Therefore the prayer for the unity of the churches of God is an absolute precondition for any discussion of doctrine and any resolution of differences.

These two principles form the heart of everything that follows in this paper.

Worship and Christian division

Throughout much of our divided Christian history, worship has frequently been the servant of our disunity. History shows us that the divisions which have separated Christians have been expressed not simply in anathemas and theological treaties. The divisions have been expressed in and through worship. When differences in teaching could not be reconciled and when differences in practice were no longer acceptable, division was manifest in worship. Altar was set up against altar, congregation was pitted against congregation, preacher was set against preacher.

With the development of division, worship became not an expression of the unity of God's people in Christ through the Spirit, but a very visible and tangible expression of irreconcilable differences. Worship became the context in which our doctrinal differences were received and "celebrated". Worship became an expression of estrangement.

This does not mean that unity demands uniformity in liturgical practices and expressions. Acceptable differences in pastoral care, theological expression and liturgical practices characterized church life prior to schisms. Yet, as schisms developed, legitimate differences in liturgical practices often took on new importance. These differences frequently came to express the differences between divided Christians. The type of bread used in the eucharist, for example, was almost raised to the level of doctrine in the eleventh-century discussions between Rome and Constantinople.

It is important to remember that for many unschooled in formal theology the liturgical differences also came to express the distinctiveness of separated churches or denominations. Should the eucharistic bread be leavened or unleavened? Should children be baptized or should baptized children receive communion? Should the wine be mixed or unmixed? Should our prayer be structured or free? Should icons be venerated or not? Should icons, statues or crosses be used in churches? Should we pray before an altar-table or before a pulpit?

Indeed, each of the great divisions in Christian history have produced different emphases in liturgical practice and worship. As with doctrinal positions, these liturgical emphases often came as a reaction to a perceived abuse or distortion. However, the liturgical "correction" was itself a "reaction" which often lacked a sensitivity to deeper issues of liturgical life. The loss of a sense of catholicity did little to advance the cause of liturgical renewal at times of estrangement.

Throughout the course of much of our divided Christian history, therefore, the actions and words of Christians in worship frequently expressed our differences and "celebrated" our disunity. Theological discussions about particular practices or particular abuses were coloured by the polemics of the time. Yes, our worship has been, and continues to be, contaminated by the tragedy of our divisions.

Worship and Christian unity

It is truly a blessing that the contemporary ecumenical movement has recognized and affirmed, in some measure, the value of prayer for reconciliation and unity. This emphasis upon common prayer for unity has very visibly challenged the complacency of our disunity. For many Christians of our generations, the special prayer services offered during the Week of Prayer for Christian Unity provided the first opportunity to gather with Christians of other churches and traditions for worship.

Over the past three decades especially, other opportunities for special prayer services for unity have also become popular in various places. In the United States, for example, it is common for Orthodox, Catholic and Protestant parishes to participate not only in the Week of Prayer in January but also in the World Day of Prayer in March as well as in special services held during Lent, at Pentecost, at Thanksgiving and during Advent.

I know that some of us may take these ecumenical prayer services for granted. We have become accustomed to them. Yet I would remind you that fifty years ago it would have been impossible for all our parents, despite their best intentions, to meet in the same chapel and even say the Lord's prayer together. With this fact in mind let us ask ourselves, what is the significance of these special ecumenical services of prayer? I would highlight six points for your consideration.

First, let us be reminded that authentic prayer and worship have an intrinsic value which cannot be diminished or forgotten. Through prayer, we respond in thanksgiving and praise to the Father, through the Son, in the Spirit. This response opens us up to be conformed by the Spirit to Christ who leads us to the Father. All authentic prayer has an intrinsic value and worth.

Second, ecumenical prayer services remind us that not all the bonds of unity have been broken. Ecumenical prayer services bring together divided Christians to pray for the restoration of full communion. Despite our divisions, we do share some measure of distinctive communion with all those who are baptized in Christ. In offering praise and thanksgiving to God, we have a special intention that full communion will be restored.

Third, these ecumenical prayer services have encouraged divided Christians to move beyond the isolation of their particular parish or denominations. Many Christians today have come to discover traditions of worship which are different from their own. In some measure, these services have opened divided Christians to a wider and richer perception of Christianity.

Fourth, these ecumenical services have helped make Christians more comfortable in attending other services and sacraments in churches other than their own. In some measure, the pain of Christian divisions in many families has been alleviated because it is possible to attend baptisms, weddings and funerals held in another church.

Participation in these services has also produced another important consequence. Many have discovered the profound similarities in the structure of the services and often the language of the prayers. Many have been able to participate together in prayers offered in their common language. The liturgical renewal movement and the ecumenical work of liturgical scholars has in fact found expression in parish life. And all of this has had a bearing upon the movement towards full communion.

Fifth, these ecumenical prayer services have intensified the question of "intercommunion" or "eucharistic hospitality". The fundamental question is this: If we can pray together, then why can we not receive holy communion together? It is a question which reflects the advances not only in the ecumenical movement but also in the liturgical and parish renewal movements. This means that the question of the sharing in communion between divided Christians has a serious dimension which was not present only a few decades ago.

Sixth, these ecumenical prayer services have also contributed to strengthening Christian witness in a given place. Prayer for reconciliation and unity can lead to a desire for united Christian witness and service. There is a profound spiritual connection between Christians praying together and Christians serving together in the name of Christ.

I am fully aware that these positive perspectives of ecumenical prayer services are conditioned by the context in which I have lived and served as an Orthodox pastor and theologian. I am fully aware of the difficulties which many of our churches face in relating to each other in some parts of the world. The issues of Christian division continue to contribute to pain and suffering today in many lands. It is important, therefore, that those of us who have experienced some measure of reconciliation both in prayer and in dialogue bear witness to this fact all the more.

Ecumenical prayer services are helping to prepare Christian people to receive the statements of reconciliation and unity. These prayers are nurturing a spirit of reconciliation which must be present at the parish level. Reconciliation among Christians will be multi-dimensional. The spirit of reconciliation among Christians in the local parishes will enrich the work of theologians. And likewise, the work of theologians who craft the documents of agreement must enrich those in the local parishes. We do not know what lies ahead in the mysterious process of reconciliation. Yet it would seem safe to assume that the spirit of reconciliation must be central to every dimension of church life.

Some concerns

My positive evaluation must be tempered by some concerns which I consider to be very serious. These concerns have to do with tendencies which I believe could easily diminish the advances which have already been made in the area of common prayer.

I am troubled that issues of prayer and spirituality do not always receive sufficient attention in the ecumenical agenda of ecumenical organizations. Perhaps in some measure this reflects the fact that many of our churches have not sufficiently emphasized the importance of spirituality. Perhaps it reflects the fact that many of us, theologians and church administrators, have not cultivated spiritual disciplines in our own life.

I am troubled that our ecumenical prayer services are frequently dominated and driven by issues which not only deflect from the concern for Christian unity and reconciliation but also become the focus of the service.

Christian worship, even ecumenical Christian worship, must always be worship. This means that it must be most fundamentally a response to the presence and actions of the Father, in Christ through the Spirit. Yes, within the context of our worship, we certainly have the opportunity to lift up our concerns in prayer. But when our concerns become the dominant element of the actions and words, than it seems that Christian worship has been transmuted into something else entirely.

I am troubled by the fact that some ecumenical prayer services are losing their grounding in the Christian tradition. In an effort to be "inclusive" and not to offend certain participants, the Christian essence and content of these services are being compromised. Here I am speaking about the intentional distortion of scripture and the intentional distortion of Trinitarian language in prayer and hymns. There is an intimate relationship between "the rule of faith" and "the rule of prayer". What we say or do not say in our prayer reflects what we believe or do not believe.

For many of us, participation in ecumenical prayer services has been predicated upon the fact that the fundamental convictions of the apostolic faith continue to be expressed through the scripture and the prayer and the hymns of the worshipping community. When these fundamental convictions of the apostolic faith are lacking or are intentionally distorted, then many of us will have to choose not to participate in such services of prayer.

I pray that this crisis can be averted.

Spirituality and unity

My emphasis thus far has been on the importance of praying together even though we continue to be divided. May I conclude with two observations which relate to the broader issue of spirituality and Christian unity.

First, we need to be very attentive to the way that we approach the issues of Christian division. The great issues which have divided Christians for centuries need to be addressed in their entirety. We cannot ignore this obligation regardless of how painful or frustrating this may be at times. But these issues cannot be addressed without reference to the present, as we relate to the Triune God as believers today. We cannot ignore the fact that our prayers together have changed us, have changed the situations of our churches, and have changed, in many cases, the way we approach the classical issues of division.

In the past our predecessors, and in fact many of us, have approached the issues of Christian division more as lawyers, or as politicians, or as military strategists or as diplomats. We have often borrowed the models of law or government and applied them to the issues of Christian division. We may, in fact, have something to learn from these models. Yet they are not fully applicable to the issues of Christian division, chiefly because they lack a rootedness in the gospel. In the final analysis, we are called not to be lawyers and politicians but pastors, theologians, and "friends of God". Here I am reminded of the description of Evagrius of Pontus who said: "A theologian is one who truly prays. And one who truly prays is a theologian."

We can choose the manner in which we approach the issues of division. We can choose the way in which we do our theological reflection. We can choose the manner in which we relate to those with whom we dialogue. These divisions will be healed if we truly approach them with the "mind of Christ" (1 Cor. 2:16). This means that we must be ever sensitive to the fact that we are called to speak about the reality of the Triune God in the present, and always with honesty, humility, sensitivity and love which reflect the presence of Christ in our midst.

Second, the relationship between spirituality and Christian unity also has a bearing upon the issue of reception, the reception of doctrinal agreements. The divisions which afflict Christianity today are not simply the result of terminological misunderstandings and doctrinal differences compounded by historical and cultural factors. Our divisions also result from a type of spiritual blindness which manifests itself in pride, arrogance, self-righteousness, and the lack of love. Earlier in this paper, I spoke of this as "hardness of heart".

This means that the restoration of full communion between churches will be accomplished not simply through formal doctrinal agreements crafted by theologians. Again I wish to emphasize the importance of theological dialogue. But while these formal agreements are extremely important, something else is also required.

There have been many important moments in the early history of the church when serious divisions have been healed. A restoration of unity follows the Arian crisis of the fourth century and is centred upon the council of Constantinople in 381. The historic Nicene-Constantinopolitan Creed bears witness to this reconciliation. A restoration of unity between the church of Alexandria and the church of Antioch in 433 is expressed in a letter of Patriarch Cyril and Patriarch John. A restoration of unity between the church of Rome and the church of Constantinople also centres upon a statement expressed by the Council of 879.

When I examine these documents of reconciliation, I am struck by a few simple facts. These statements are quite brief — despite the great debates which usually preceded them. The statements are not major analytical documents. Rather, they have a strong doxological character.

These documents tell me that something else happened! These events of reconciliation were not simply the result of finding the "right words". The documents do not create unity. Rather, it seems that the documents bear witness to a deeper reality which the words do not capture fully. While the words of reconciliation were important, the attitude of the heart of those who fashioned the words and those who received them is of greater importance. Behind each of these historic statements of reconciliation are persons who became open to the prodding of the Holy Spirit, not simply in their minds but in their hearts as well.

The restoration of unity in our time will be accomplished gradually and in a most fundamental way when our statements of reconciliation are both fashioned and received by persons who are first of all open to the presence and activity of the Holy Spirit. And this openness to the "giver of life" will not simply be expressed in words! It will be expressed in prayerful metanoia, in the healing of memories, in acts of forgiveness, and in a renewed commitment together to the Lord and his gospel.

To him be glory together with the eternal Father and the all holy, good and life giving Spirit: now and forever and unto ages of ages. Amen.

NOTE

[1] PG 87, 2985.

Liturgical Inculturation and the Search for Unity

ANSCAR J. CHUPUNGCO, O.S.B.

The questions we need to ask

The topic I was assigned to discuss at this ecumenical consultation is a complex and challenging matter: what are the implications of inculturation for our common search for liturgical unity, and what are the criteria and limits imposed by Christian worship on inculturation? Inculturation by its nature and inner dynamics tends to diversify or lead to a pluralism of cultural expressions in the liturgy. Among the many things that bind together mainstream Christian churches is the liturgical culture they still share across their differences in doctrine and discipline. In the West they continue to preserve the layers of cultural tradition the Western church inherited from Judaism, the Greco-Roman world, and the Franco-Germanic empire. What effect will inculturation have on this?

It seems to me that there are foundational questions an ecumenical forum needs to raise, as it strives after unity in liturgical worship within the context of cultural diversity. In this regard, I can think of three leading questions, though there are probably more.

The first question refers to the cultural unity of the different Christian confessions. We know that when the great reformers of the sixteenth century worked to curb the abuses that crept into the medieval church of the West, they did not abandon the cultural heritage of the Western church. Reformed ways of celebrating the liturgy were introduced, but the underlying cultural patterns remained unaltered. The liturgical formularies, though recited in the vernacular, continued to be Greco-Roman in style, while in many a church the institutions and symbols of Franco-Germanic origin persisted. Most of all the Jewish roots of the liturgy of the word, baptism and the Lord's supper remained intact. If inculturation, as I said earlier, brings about a diversity of cultural expressions, will it not adversely affect the cultural unity that still binds the various Christian churches across confessional differences? In effect, will not inculturation abandon the cultural unity the Reformation tried to preserve?

The second question concerns the local communities that make up a church. When people speak of the liturgy of the Roman Catholic Church, the Anglican communion, or the Reformed churches, they normally refer to the practices, however loosely observed, that hold these churches together and distinguish them from one another. It is not unusual that the founding church from Europe or North America hands on its liturgy, which is identifiably Western, to the new church in Africa, Latin America, or Asia. Thus both mother and daughter churches normally share the same cultural tradition in worship. But when a daughter church inculturates the liturgy, will unity with the mother church not become less evident? On the other hand, will it not come about that in the same country or region the resemblance among local churches belonging to different confessions will be closer because they share a common cultural expression?

The third question deals with culture. The liturgy as action of a concrete ecclesial community is by necessity a cultural reality. Christian worship, both in its language and rites, is so inextricably bound up with the culture of a people, that it is not possible to celebrate it outside a cultural context or in a cultural vacuum. No community, after all, exists in a cultural vacuum. History itself attests to the incorporation into the liturgy of elements of practically every culture with which the church has come into contact. This explains the different layers of culture that are present in Christian worship. The question that occupies us here is whether everything and anything cultural, provided it is not diametrically opposed to the gospel message, may be assimilated by the liturgy. Does not the liturgy have its own requirements that ultimately determine the limits of inculturation? And on the part of culture, does it not have its own laws and dynamics which should be respected in the process of assimilating its elements into the liturgy? In short, can we define the rules to be observed when Christian worship enters into dialogue with culture?

A definition of inculturation

To assist our common reflection, allow me to review the meaning of liturgical inculturation, namely what it is and what it is not. John Paul II has defined inculturation as "an intimate transformation of the authentic cultural values by their integration into Christianity and the implantation of Christianity into different human cultures".[1] Applied to liturgical worship, the definition implies several things.

First, inculturation as a dialogue between liturgy and culture is marked by the spirit of respect for what is honest, beautiful and noble in human culture. The early Christian writers, while condemning the moral decadence of their time, showed eagerness to incorporate suitable cultural elements into church worship. We know that the rites of Christian initiation developed through the assimilation of practices in common use during the early centuries. Examples are anointing, the giving of a white garment and lighted candle, foot-washing, and the offering of a cup of milk and honey to neophytes.

Second, inculturation means that the cultural elements adopted by the liturgy are so integrated with the texts and rites of worship that they become con-natural vehicles of the liturgical message. In other words, inculturation is not juxtaposition of unassimilated elements or a mere external adaptation. The early models of liturgical inculturation were truly a work of genius. Proof of this is that today the uninitiated has difficulty to identify the elements Christian liturgy borrowed from the Jewish, Greco-Roman, Franco-Germanic and late medieval European cultures. The plan of the liturgy of the word, for example, is synagogal: the rite of marriage is basically typical of an early Roman ceremony; and the act of contrition still in use among a number of churches was influenced by the Franco-Germanic "apologies".

And third, inculturation leads to mutual enrichment. Culture is evangelized as it comes in contact with the gospel message the church proclaims during worship. Evangelization results from the critique made by the gospel on culture, a critique that implies correction of defective values or even outright rejection of ideas and practices that by their very nature are incompatible or inconsistent with the gospel message. Evangelization also results from the incorporation of cultural elements into the liturgy. In this way they are elevated to a superior sphere, they are integrated into the saving act of God. The early church normally reinterpreted them in the light of the Old and New Testaments. For example, the third-century *Apostolic Tradition*, a book attributed to Hippolytus of Rome, interprets the practice of giving the cup of milk and honey to neophytes during communion as the fulfilment of God's promise that he would lead his chosen people to a land flowing with milk and honey. In reality ancient Romans had the practice of giving the same drink to newly-born infants for strength and as protection against evil spirits. The liturgical practice seems to have been derived from this, but its meaning underwent a reorientation. Today we call this method biblical typology. The long and short of it is that before the church incorporates cultural elements into the liturgy, it critiques them first by evaluating them in the light of the gospel message.

Christian worship itself is enriched by the culture it embraces. Baptism as "the washing of water with the word" (Eph. 5:26) would surely be complete by itself. But today who would deny that the other rites added in the course of time to the washing of water with the word have greatly enhanced our appreciation of the sacrament? The first disciples' "breaking of bread in their homes" (Acts 2:46) tells us a great deal about the eucharist, but Justin Martyr's second-century report on the liturgy of the word preceding the Lord's supper, the seventh-century addition of imperial court ceremonials, and the Lutheran inclusion of hymns have surely enriched our eucharistic celebration.

From a theological point of view we may regard the process of inculturation as a consequence of the mystery of the incarnation. Indeed the incarnation of the Son of God is the paradigm or model of inculturation. Just as Christ became human in all things, save sin, and bound himself with the culture and tradition of his people, so the church is tasked to extend the incarnation in time and space. This it accomplishes by assimilating suitable components of human culture in its preaching, worship and works of service to humankind, so that Christ's message may be grafted on the culture and traditions of peoples. Understood in this light, inculturation is not an option but an imperative, for through it Christ breaks into the life and history of nations.

> By inculturation, the church makes the gospel incarnate in different cultures, and at the same time introduces peoples, together with their cultures, into its own community.[2]

From an anthropological point of view we may regard liturgical inculturation as a dialogue between Christian worship and culture. Dialogue is carried out concretely in the context of the three components of culture, namely values, patterns and institutions. These are the things with which the liturgy holds dialogue, and hence should be closely examined by those who are engaged in the work of inculturation.

Allow me briefly to recall what I have written on this topic for a liturgy consultation organized by the Lutheran World Federation.[3] Values are principles which influence and direct the life of a community. They form the community's basic behaviour towards religious, political and ethical realities. Some of the notable human values which dialogue with Christian worship are family or community spirit, leadership and hospitality. Patterns, on the other hand, are the typical and hence predictable way members of a society form concepts, express thoughts in language and the arts, and celebrate various aspects of life. The language pattern of the Roman people from the fifth to the seventh century, which was characterized by rhetoric, deeply influenced the corpus of the Roman liturgical formularies. Likewise the ritual pattern of ancient Rome known for its sobriety and practicality left an appreciable mark on the Roman liturgical *ordo*. Lastly, institutions are society's traditional rites of passage from birth to death. Initiatory rites, the rites of marriage and parenthood, leadership rites, and rites connected with sickness, death and funerals fall under this category. Other institutions are celebrations to mark the passing of the seasons or the anniversary of legends and memorable historical events. Institutions have dominated the interest of the church, as we can gather from the great number of liturgical rites and feasts which originate in the rites of passage and the festivals.

In summary, allow me to point out the basic concepts related to liturgical inculturation. These are: dialogue between Christian worship and cultural values, patterns and institutions; the assimilation and integration of pertinent cultural elements into the liturgy; and the theological dynamic of the incarnation.

The limits of liturgical inculturation

I have outlined what inculturation is, but what is it not? Or in other words, what are its limits? First, it is not that particular type of creative activity which stems purely from one's rich imagination, fantasy or personal preferences. Inculturation is rooted in the living and received liturgical tradition of one's church; it begins with the actual praxis or else is based on tradition. That is why it does not produce alternative liturgies that are not backed by tradition or praxis. The practical implication of this is that the work of inculturation should be preceded by a careful study of the received tradition and actual praxis of the liturgy. In this sense creativity is an easier and often more entertaining endeavour than inculturation. One who is not familiar with the tradition of one's church or ignores its practices is bound to render an immense disservice to the liturgy and to inculturation.

Second, inculturation should not become a form of cultural imposition. While we should respect what is honest and noble in every culture, not everything we find good in culture can be assimilated into the liturgy. Cultural elements should not only be beyond doctrinal or moral reproach, they should also possess that quality which I call the "con-naturality" to express the meaning and purpose of Christian worship. Thus it is not enough that we do not impose on the liturgy such cultural values, patterns and institutions as will obscure or perhaps deny the church's received tradition and actual praxis. We should also fulfil the condition that said cultural components are integrated with Christian worship and that they do not remain as tokens or worse as alien bodies that have absolutely nothing to do with the liturgy.

Third, there are limits to inculturation set down by the liturgy itself. These are principles or requirements that emerge from the nature and purpose of the liturgy. Allow me to review them here. For reference I use two documents. These are the Faith and Order text "Worship and the Oneness of Christ's Church",[4] and the text of the Roman Catholic Church, "The Roman Liturgy and Inculturation".[5] It is heartening to note that the two documents are in agreement on what constitutes the essence of Christian worship, and hence on the boundary beyond which inculturation would be an encroachment on the liturgy and a threat to the fundamental unity in worship among Christian churches. Inculturation, I noted earlier, tends to diversify liturgical expressions among local communities even within the same confession because of cultural differences. These two documents define the limits beyond which diversity, brought about by cultural assimilation, can undermine that basic liturgical unity among the churches.

It is not possible to develop at this point the liturgical principles contained in the two documents. But a quick enumeration might be useful. First, the Vatican Instruction, repeating the conciliar Constitution on the Liturgy,[6] teaches that the liturgy is at once the action of Christ the priest and of the church his body, which he continually associates with himself in the work of redemption. Or as the Montreal report puts it:

> By him, with him and in him who is our great High Priest and Intercessor we offer to the Father, in the power of the Holy Spirit, our praise, thanksgiving and intercession.[7]

Hence, the liturgy is a sacred action which cannot be reduced to a socio-cultural activity. A pattern of celebration that is purely horizontal in language and rites forgets that the liturgy is the privileged moment when Christians meet God through Christ in the Holy Spirit.

Second, the liturgy is always the anamnesis of the mystery of Jesus Christ, a mystery which culminated in his death, resurrection, and sending of the Holy Spirit to the church. The Montreal report explains that

> Christian worship, set forth in baptism and celebrated in the eucharist, is grounded and centred in the historical ministry of Jesus Christ, his death and resurrection, and his exalted and continuing ministry.[8]

Christian liturgy by definition is Christocentric. That is why the celebrations of a mythical story or legend, an important event in political history, or a nature festival can become part of Christian worship only after they have been purified and integrated with the mystery of Christ.

Third, the liturgy is an ecclesial gathering of the priestly people who respond in faith to God's gratuitous call. According to the Montreal report,

> Christian worship, as a participation in Christ's own self-offering, is an act formative of Christian community — an act, moreover, which is conducted within the context of the whole Church, and which represents the one, catholic Church.[9]

In the words of the Vatican Instruction on inculturation:

> Because it is *catholic*, the Church overcomes the barriers which divide humanity: by Baptism all become children of God and form in Christ Jesus one people where "there is neither Jew nor Greek, neither slave nor free, neither male nor female" (Gal. 3:28). Thus the Church is called to gather all peoples, to speak all languages, to penetrate all cultures.[10]

The liturgy should therefore mirror the catholicity of the church, a catholicity that knows no barriers, no "social division based on class, race or nation".[11] Such a liturgy, because it is hospitable and welcoming, is a powerful critique of socio-cultural systems that deny human equality and, alas, the dignity of the poor and the lowly.

Fourth, the catholicity of the liturgy also means that it is celebrated "in the context of the whole church" and that it "represents the one, catholic church". This is elaborated by the Vatican Instruction in these words:

> The Church of Christ is made present and signified, in a given place and in a given time, by the local or particular Churches which through the liturgy reveal the Church in its true nature. That is why every particular Church must be united with the universal Church not only in belief and sacramentals, but also in those practices received through the Church as part of the uninterrupted apostolic tradition.[12]

Inculturation should not cause the fragmentation of the church nor of its worship. What it should aim for is to allow variations in the cultural expression of the same liturgical tradition and praxis, not departure from these. Inculturation is basically the faithful translation into different but suitable cultural values, patterns and institutions of what the churches have received from the apostles. Hence, inculturation does not break unity nor does it introduce practices that are totally alien from the gospel message. This brings us back to our initial question: how deeply do we know and appreciate the liturgical tradition and praxis of the church?

Fifth, the Montreal report explains that

> Christian worship in the form of preaching is based upon the commandment of Jesus Christ and his promise that he himself will be present with the hearers, working in them by his word.[13]

This same thought is repeated by the Vatican Instruction:

> The Church is nourished on the word of God written in the Old and New Testaments. When the Church proclaims the word in the liturgy, it welcomes it as a way in which Christ is present: "it is he who speaks when the Sacred Scriptures are read in Church".[14]

The practical implications of this are outlined for us in the same Instruction. First, the holy scripture must not be replaced by any other text, no matter how venerable it may be. The temptation to do so is felt strongly when a people is in possession of sacred writings which are not canonically recognized by Christian churches. Second, the Bible is the indispensable source of the liturgy's language, of its signs, and of its prayers especially in the psalms. Inculturation does not mean that the liturgy will dispense with biblical language and symbols. What it means is that efforts will be made to translate and transmit them into the equivalent language and symbols of a people.

Sixth, to borrow the lapidary words of the Montreal report,

> Christian worship is at once remembrance, communion and expectation. It points beyond the present moment to the tasks of Christian witness which lie before us, as we join in Christ's ministry to the world, and as we look for the consummation of God's kingdom; for this side of that kingdom all our doings in the church are but a partial anticipation of the glory which is to come.[15]

The same idea is repeated by the Vatican Instruction:

> The church is a pilgrim on earth far from the Lord, it bears the marks of the present time in the sacraments and in its institutions, but is waiting in joyful hope for the coming of Jesus Christ. This is expressed in the prayers of petition: it shows that we are citizens of heaven, who are at the same time attentive to the needs of humanity and of society.[16]

Liturgy is both expectation of the future glory and dedication to the work of building the earthly city in the image of the heavenly. Thus, Christian worship is a sharp critique to a world that regards material progress as the ultimate aim of history. In the liturgy we proclaim that there is another side to human life. At the same time we Christians are invited by the liturgy to involve ourselves in the human struggle for justice, peace and true progress. The liturgy is not a kind of opium that makes Christians insensitive to the sad plight of humankind. Inculturation should not obscure these two fundamental aspects of Christian worship.

Inculturation: towards diversity in unity

If we understand inculturation as a form of dynamic translation and not as pure creativity, we have little to fear that it will impinge on the unity of the churches in the area of worship. Authentic inculturation does not create new liturgies; rather, it translates culturally what each of the churches has received and nurtures. The aim of inculturation is to graft liturgical texts and rites on the culture of the local worshipping community. Thus, it paves the way towards diversity of cultural expressions in the unity of tradition and praxis.

The question is, how does it work? How does one go about inculturating the liturgy? What adequate methods are available? If we examine both the historical and contemporary models of inculturation, we arrive at the conclusion that there are in fact several methods available. Among them the method of dynamic equivalence merits particular attention, because it is partial to the preservation of unity.

Dynamic equivalence consists of replacing components of the liturgy with something in the local culture that has an equal meaning or value. Through this method the linguistic, ritual, and symbolic patterns of the liturgy are re-expressed in the corresponding patterns of the local community. This is what the word "equivalence" involves. This method brings about a culturally evocative liturgy whose language, rites and symbols admirably relate to the community of worship, as they evoke life experiences and traditions and paint vivid images of creation and history. This is what the word "dynamic" means.

Something to remember about the method of dynamic equivalence is that it is intrinsically and basically a work of translation, albeit dynamic. Because it is a work of translation rather than the creation of new liturgies, it is able to preserve unity across the diversity of cultural expressions.

We are faced here with two questions, namely in what does liturgical unity consist and what is in fact translated? For the Roman Catholic Church the answer has been officially given, though it appears to be rather restrictive. According to the Vatican Instruction cited above,

> the process of inculturation should maintain the *substantial unity* of the Roman rite. This unity is currently expressed in the typical editions of liturgical books, published by authority of the Supreme Pontiff, and in the liturgical books approved by the Episcopal Conferences for their areas and confirmed by the Apostolic See.[17]

For the Roman Catholic Church, then, inculturation is primarily the translation of the official liturgical books into the living culture and traditions of the local churches.

Not all churches possess a typical edition of liturgical books similar to that of the Roman Catholic Church. However, I presume that each one has a received rite of baptism, a praxis common to its member churches, a particular way of administering baptism, or in short a baptismal *ordo*, however loosely such an *ordo* might be observed by local churches. The same can probably be said, by and large, of the rite for celebrating the eucharist. Such *ordines* are, in their own right, official books or points of reference for the entire church. It seems to me that even in the absence of typical editions or a received rite the method of dynamic equivalence can produce satisfactory results in terms of inculturated liturgy and the preservation of liturgical unity. What inspires me to make this affirmation is the Montreal report which records the general agreement among different confessions on the celebration of baptism and the eucharist.

Regarding the rite of baptism, the report announces that "we have found general agreement that the following elements should find a place within any comprehensive order of baptism".[18] The underpinning principle of liturgical unity being proposed here is not largely different from the principle of unity articulated in the Roman typical editions, except that these tend to be ritually detailed and concrete. In other words, across their confessional differences the churches share certain elements that constitute a baptismal *ordo*. These elements embody the basic liturgical unity among churches of different confessions, a unity that transcends the details of a typical or official edition of the baptismal rite. What the method of dynamic equivalence aims to do is to translate these elements of liturgical unity to the culture of the local churches.

The Montreal report names seven of these elements:

- an acknowledgment of God's initiative in salvation, of his continuing faithfulness, and of our total dependence on his grace;
- a declaration of the forgiveness of sins in and through Christ;
- an invocation of the Holy Spirit;
- a renunciation of evil;
- a profession of faith in Christ;
- an affirmation that the person baptized is a child of God and is incorporated into the body of Christ, whereby he or she becomes a witness of the gospel; and
- the baptism with water in the name of the Father and of the Son and of the Holy Spirit.[19]

These are the elements that express the liturgical unity enjoyed by the churches on the question of baptism. They are in effect also the elements that are translated through the method of dynamic equivalence. I have intentionally reproduced them here in order to underline the concepts that are culturally well disposed and hence friendly to the process of dynamic translation. These concepts are: acknowledgment, declaration, invocation, renunciation, profession, affirmation, incorporation and witnessing. We know that every culture has a particular, perhaps unique, way of expressing them in language, gestures and symbols. Dynamic equivalence means that the rite of baptism, which includes these elements, is elaborated in such a way as to re-express in the culture and traditions of the local community the shared elements of baptism. No element is lost in the process. Hence, the basic unity is not broken. In other words, God's initiative in salvation is acknowledged, forgiveness of sins is declared, the Holy Spirit is invoked, evil is renounced, and so on: but these constitutive elements of baptism are now re-expressed in the context of the values, patterns and institutions of the people.

As regards the rite for the eucharistic celebration, the Montreal report names the "usual", which are also the traditional, components, namely a service of the word and a service of the sacrament. The report says that the service of the word contains the reading and preaching of the word and the intercession of the whole church and for the world. The service of the sacrament, on the other hand, has a shape determined by the actions of our Lord at the last supper: taking bread and wine to be used by God in this service; blessing God for creation and redemption and invoking the Holy Spirit, reciting the words of institution, and saying the Lord's prayer; breaking the bread; and giving the bread and the wine in communion. The report mentions other important though secondary themes. Among them are the expression of contrition, the recitation of the creed, the celebration of the communion of saints, and the announcement of the Lord's coming.[20]

What the Montreal report has described is basically a eucharistic *ordo* of long-standing tradition. It is almost identical with the plan of the eucharist mentioned in the second-century *First Apology* of Justin Martyr. The typical or official editions have done nothing else but elaborate this basic and detailed plan which is a common possession of the churches. Again inculturation does not mean to offer a totally new alternative plan based perhaps on types of meals found in various cultural traditions. What it does through dynamic equivalence is translate the elements of the received eucharistic rite. Thus, it is the word of God that is proclaimed and preached and prayed upon, but according to a suitable pattern of proclamation and intercession found in a given culture. Thus, God is blessed for the work of creation and redemption in Jesus Christ, but the pattern of blessing corresponds to a particular culture. Thus, too, the eucharistic bread and wine are given to the assembly, but the pattern of distribution evokes a local culture.

Summary

With the foregoing exposition, which I realize is more of a hasty synthesis than a deliberate discussion, it was my intention to underline the premises for inculturation, if it is to become an instrument of evangelization and liturgical unity among churches and their members.

These premises can be summarized as follows. First, we need to know what are the received traditions and actual praxis of our particular churches and how they relate to the general convictions of other churches. The Montreal report together with the Vatican instruction on inculturation are most helpful in registering the basic agreement of the churches on the nature of Christian worship and the celebration of baptism and the eucharist. As the Montreal report so aptly said,

> it is of crucial importance that we should investigate its [worship's] forms and structures, its language and spirit, in the expectation that this process may throw new light upon various theological positions and affirmations, perhaps even lend new meaning to them, and thus open new possibilities in ecumenical dialogue.[21]

A second premise is the need to study the nature of inculturation together with its dynamics and its methods. We should not tire of repeating that inculturation is not absolute creativity but dynamic translation of our inherited traditions and actual praxis. It does not ignore them but rather builds on them, elaborates them, re-expresses them. Alas, it sometimes happens that people subject the liturgy to personal whims in the name of inculturation, and thus unknowingly break the liturgical unity of the churches.

Lastly, we need to examine closely our own local cultures composed of values, patterns and institutions, and how these can suitably be integrated into Christian worship after due critique and purification. While we must respect culture and traditions, we realize that not everything they offer suit the nature and purpose of Christian worship. Inculturation, in other words, is selective as to the elements it incorporates into the liturgy.

Allow me to conclude this paper with the remarkable words which Paul VI addressed to the members of the commission he appointed to review the Roman rite after Vatican Council II. They are words that encourage us to welcome the promptings of the Holy Spirit, as we search for cultural diversity in worship within the context of our common tradition. He told them:

> The voice of the Church today must not be so constricted that she could not sing a new song, should the inspiration of the Holy Spirit move her to do so.[22]

NOTES

[1] *Redemptoris missio*, 1990, no. 52.

[2] *Ibid.*

[3] "Liturgy and the Components of Culture", *Worship and Culture in Dialogue*, ed. S. Anita Stauffer, LWF Studies, Geneva, Lutheran World Federation, 1994, pp.153-66.

[4] *The Fourth World Conference on Faith and Order: Montreal 1963*, eds P.C. Rodger & L. Vischer, Faith and Order Paper no. 42, London, SCM, 1964, pp.69-75.

[5] IVth Instruction for the Right Application of the Conciliar Constitution on the Liturgy (nn.37-40), in *Osservatore Romano*, 14 April 1994.

[6] No. 7.

[7] *The Fourth World Conference, op. cit.*, pp.73-74.

[8] *Ibid.*, p.71.

[9] *Ibid.*, p.70.

[10] IVth Instruction, *op. cit.*, no. 22.

[11] *The Fourth World Conference*, *op. cit.*, p.70.

[12] IVth Instruction, *op. cit.*, no. 26.

[13] *The Fourth World Conference*, *op. cit.*, p.70.

[14] IVth Instruction, *op. cit.*, no. 23.

[15] *The Fourth World Conference*, *op. cit.*

[16] IVth Instruction, *op. cit.*, no. 22.

[17] *Ibid.*, no. 36.

[18] *The Fourth World Conference*, *op. cit.*, p.72.

[19] *Ibid.*

[20] *Ibid.*, p.74.

[21] *Ibid.*, p.70.

[22] Allocution of 13 October 1966, published in English in *Documents on the Liturgy 1963-1979: Conciliar, Papal and Curial Texts*, International Commission on English in the Liturgy, Collegeville, Minnesota, Liturgical Press, 1982, document no. 84, pp.223-26, see p.224.

Worship and Culture

S. ANITA STAUFFER

How can worship be both truly Christian and truly Namibian, or both truly Christian and truly Chinese, or both truly Christian and truly Sami? How can worship be both authentic to its Judeo-Christian roots, and relevant in each culture of today's world? What are the linguistic styles and images which can be used in preaching, and in liturgical texts, in given cultural settings, so that worship is meaningful to the people there? What are the aesthetics of a given culture, and how does the aesthetic system relate to a sense of the holy for the people there? What are the musical styles and architectural prototypes in a given culture, and how can they be adapted for Christian worship?

In an attempt to explore such questions as these, in 1992 the office for worship of the Lutheran World Federation initiated a long-term interdisciplinary study of worship and culture. This study project, which is to examine church music and church architecture as well as liturgy and homiletics, includes four phases. Phase I consisted of an international working group of scholars, with two meetings and publication of the papers and report. Phase II involves research by regional and sub-regional study teams in the five continents of the world. Phase III will have a consultation of the international study team, with publication of the report. Phase IV is planned to consist of seminars in the regions and churches.

This study team is a diverse group. It includes a sociologist from south India; a Chinese musician; a specialist in African music; a Swedish architect; bishops from Chile and Slovakia; a systematic theologian from Papua New Guinea; liturgics professors from seminaries in Japan, Brazil, the Central African Republic, and the United States; the Church of Norway staff person for the Sami people; parish pastors from Ethiopia, Canada and Argentina; a university chaplain from South Africa; and worship staff persons from LWF member churches in Sweden, Germany and the United States. Because the issues and questions are shared across confessional lines, the study team has ecumenical participation, with representatives from the Roman Catholic Church, the Anglican Communion, the World Methodist Council, and the World Council of Churches.

The two major resource people are the Rev. Dr Gordon Lathrop, eminent New Testament scholar and Lutheran liturgical theologian from the United States; and the Rev. Dr Anscar Chupungco, O.S.B., a Roman Catholic from the Philippines who is a leading world scholar in liturgical inculturation.

The study builds on previous work of the LWF Department for Theology and Studies, particularly the "Confessing Christ in Cultural Contexts" study of 1975-83, the Crêt-Bérard consultation and statement *(A Lutheran Agenda for Worship)* of 1979, the Tantur seminar on "The Significance of the Jewish Heritage for the Task of Contextualization" in 1981, and the work of the worship desk in the early 1980s.

The study was launched with a consultation in October 1993 in Cartigny, Switzerland, of the study team of 22 persons from 16 nations, representing every continent of the world. The study team focused on the biblical and historical foundations of the relationship between Christian worship and culture. In examining baptism and eucharist, the group explored the biblical cultures out of which Christianity developed, and then considered the dynamics of how the early church adapted its worship in the Greco-Roman and Franco-Germanic cultures in which it found itself. The relationship between worship and culture at the time of the Lutheran Reformation was also examined. Not only the texts and structures of liturgies were considered but also music and church architecture. Many of the questions churches face today are the same as those faced by early Christians, as well as in the Lutheran Reformation. Thus the group sought to learn both positive and negative lessons from ancestors in the faith.

The study team issued a statement which said:

> One helpful model, then, which is evident throughout the history of the Church, is found where the worshipping community is able to receive and use the important elements of the culture (and thus be localized in a particular context), while at the same time critically shaping these elements so that they may bear witness to the Gospel of Christ who transcends and transforms all cultures (and thus be rooted in the universal Christian tradition). "See, I am making all things new" (Rev. 21:5, NRSV).[1]

Building on its work on biblical and historical foundations, the study team met again in March 1994 in Hong Kong to focus on contemporary issues and questions of the relationships between cultures and liturgy, church music and church architecture and art. This consultation included four plenary papers, as well as seven case studies from around the globe. Prof. Mabel Wu, of the Lutheran theological seminary in Hong Kong, used two new Chinese hymns in analyzing the use of indigenous music in the context of a missionary church. The Rev. Lisandro Orlov from Argentina considered the eucharist in the Latin American context. The Rev. Louis Sibiya from South Africa reflected on baptism in the African context. The Hindu festival of Deepavali was used by Prof. Adiss Arnold of Gurukul Lutheran Theological College to consider the church year in the Indian context. The Sami people of Sweden were the focus of Dr Nils-Henrik Nilsson's case study on worship in the context of indigenous minority congregations. From Papua New Guinea, Prof. Marcus Felde reflected on the eucharist and giving thanks in a culture where there in no word for "thanks". The Rev. Eric Dyck of Canada presented a case study on worship in the context of the North American consumer and entertainment culture.[2]

The study has now moved into the regional phase, during which regional and sub-regional study teams are attempting to help LWF member churches identify and explore in depth the relationships between their own cultures and Christian worship. It is intended that the regional phase involve a wide variety of persons, including parish pastors, laity, bishops, theologians, church architects and artists, and musicians. The regional teams have been encouraged to work ecumenically to the greatest possible extent. Research methodology differs by region and sub-region. Consultations and conferences are being held in Africa, Europe and North America. Interviews are being conducted in Asia. In Latin America, a graduate-level class at the Escola Superior de Teología (Sao Leopoldo, Brazil) is being trained in both anthropology and liturgy to conduct intensive field research.

Four general areas of inquiry are included in the regional studies. (1) What cultural elements can be adapted for Christian worship (including liturgical texts, sermons, gestures, vestments, church furnishings, art, music and architecture) which can give expression to the cultural particularity of a given people? (2) What are or ought to be the counter-cultural elements in Christian worship in a given context which challenge the culture in which it is located? (3) What are the trans-cultural elements in worship which place it clearly within the universality of the Christian liturgical tradition? (4) What are the cultural riches of the church in a given context which could be shared with the global communion of churches? As the Cartigny statement said:

> Therefore, the task of relating worship and culture is ultimately concerned with finding the balance between relevance and authenticity, between particularity and universality, while avoiding eclecticism and/or syncretism. While it is clear that each church in its cultural context will need to ask these questions for itself and find answers appropriate to its own situation, it is also clear that this inquiry will require each church to attend to the experiences of the other churches and to the treasures of other cultures.[3]

The international study team will meet again in Nairobi in January 1996, to analyze and synthesize the finding of the regional studies, and to prepare for a final phase of implementation. It is hoped that as a whole, the study will foster renewal of the life of the church. As Gordon Lathrop said at the Hong Kong consultation, Lutheran churches "welcome the gifts of many cultures of the world", but "the gift of Christ" must always stand at the centre of Christian worship.

NOTES

[1] "Cartigny Statement on Worship and Culture: Biblical and Historical Foundations", in *Worship and Culture in Dialogue*, ed. S. Anita Stauffer, Geneva, LWF, 1994, para. 3.8, p.134. The complete text of the Cartigny statement is available in English, German, French and Spanish from the LWF worship desk, Department for Theology and Studies.

[2] The papers from the Cartigny and Hong Kong consultations are also included in *Worship and Culture in Dialogue*, with translations available in French, German and Spanish.

[3] "Cartigny Statement", *op. cit.*, para 3.6.

Ecumenism and Liturgy in Latin America

Reflections from Local Experiences and Examples

JACI MARASCHIN

Latin America is predominantly a Roman Catholic continent. But before Spaniards and Portuguese navigators arrived there were many indigenous cultures, in some cases with a high level of creativity and skills. Examples of this are the remains of Maya, Aztec and Aymara civilizations. They were destroyed by the Europeans, and the survivors were forced to accept, though reluctantly, the new culture with its form and substance (i.e. religion). Indigenous tribes still exist in some areas of our continent, but they are persecuted and decimated by the landlords of today. Another culture was brought especially to Brazil, but also to other countries: the African. They came in their thousands as slaves to do the hard work in the fields and mines which the white conquerors were not able to do. Today Brazilians are at least 40 percent African in origin. The Africans also brought their culture (music, religion, food, etc.) and in spite of all the disadvantages of slavery, they have succeeded in maintaining it. During the 19th century many other people immigrated to the continent, bringing also their own cultures and customs. At this moment Brazil — the easiest example for me to speak of — has a large population of Asiatics: Korean, Japanese and Chinese.

It is very hard to characterize Latin American culture. It is, indeed, a melting pot, the result of this encounter of very diversified peoples. It is misleading to think that Latin American culture is the ancient culture of the natives. Nor is it simply the marriage of black and white peoples. In the earlier years of our formation there also arrived artists and scholars from Europe, especially from France. I would venture to say that our intellectual life (as can be seen in some of our best universities) depends largely on French philosophy and culture. Of course, American and British pragmatism have also played an important role in our development.

In the beginning, Christianity was very conservative and followed the line of the teachings of Vatican I. Protestantism arrived in the last century and was also very conservative. If Roman Catholicism looked to Rome for leadership, Protestant missionaries looked to America and Britain for inspiration, and the result was a form of religion alien to the country. Also, a definite anti-ecumenism developed and there was much antipathy between groups. It was only after Vatican II that things tended to improve. The influence of the World Council of Churches was limited, and only four churches were members of this organization until very recently: Anglican, Lutheran, Methodist and another small denomination. The presence of Latin Americans in World Council of Churches gatherings is also very limited.

Nevertheless, the churches have an interest in liturgical matters and the ecumenical movement, though small, has inspired many people and congregations to experiment with new forms of worship. One of our first attempts was a seminar sponsored by the Association of Theological Schools in Brazil in 1972, where some twenty professors from Protestant seminaries in Brazil came together to discuss the meaning of worship and the place of music in it. At the same time a group of young people gave a recital of Brazilian music for worship in one of the churches in Sao Paulo. Experiments in other parts of the world also challenged our churches: I remember having been present in 1957 in a group of young people who were listening to the "20th Century Folk Mass" by Geoffrey Meaumont. Other important compositions came to Brazil like the "Missa Criolla" by Ariel Ramírez, the "Missa Luba", written in the Congo, and the "Mass of Five Melodies" from England in 1963. More recently we have had the "Missa da Nicaragua". The movement for renewal in worship had begun; many other experiments followed. In 1975 a group of poets and musicians published a book of songs entitled *A Nova Cançao* ("The New Song"); but it was a still very timid incursion into the realm of popular music for worship.

In 1979, the same association of Brazilian theological schools organized another seminar in Rio de Janeiro to study the place of song (music and lyrics) in the context of worship. Other groups joined the movement, like the Brazilian Conference of Bishops, the ecumenical centre in Rio (CEDI) and the Methodist church. The Lutheran school of theology in south Brazil also played an important role, not only by singing new songs in the chapel but also by recording them. Many books have appeared since then: *A Cançao do Senhor na Terra Brasileira* ("The Lord's Song in the Brazilian Land"), *O Novo Canto da Terra* ("The New Song of the Earth"), and *Celebraçao da Vida* ("Celebration of Life"). There are also many records and tapes.

From the Vancouver assembly of the World Council of Churches (1983) through Canberra (1990) and the Faith and Order world conference in Santiago de Compostela (1993) the presence of Latin Americans has been continuous and lively. The Vancouver worship book contained 10 songs from our continent out of 62, and one was from Brazil. Pablo Sosa from Argentina was one of the animators at the assembly and a young Brazilian was present in most of the services with his flute and trumpet. The Canberra worship book had 11 songs from Latin America, also out of 62. The worship committee and the worship leaders counted on a group of Latin Americans. The same can be said of Santiago de Compostela.

In Latin America renewal in worship has been the task of many churches and ecumenical organizations. The Latin American Council of Churches (CLAI) has given substantial support through conferences, publications and the creation of a Latin American network of liturgy, still in its beginnings. CLAI sponsored a major seminar in San José, Costa Rica, in 1988 attended by musicians and theologians from many parts of the continent. The report was entitled *Todas las Voces*.

The liturgical renewal of our churches, expressed in ecumenical meetings and organizations, follows the same lines as the international renewal. Local features are seen specifically in songs and their rhythms, and in certain dances. Compared to North Atlantic countries and cultures, Latin American culture is more colourful and physical; so it is easy to touch, to kiss, to embrace, to hold hands, to march in procession carrying banners and lights, and to express social and political visions with the symbols of our faith.

Our liturgical renewal is closely related to the theology of liberation and the struggle of our people for social, political and economic liberation. So the theme of social justice always recurs, together with the theme of hope.

However, our liturgical renewal wants to be ecumenical in a wider sense: we want to be faithful to the universal and catholic church. Our task, it seems to me, is to bring our local contribution to the global church. This is why we are interested in Gregorian chant, in the music of the Reformation, in the *kyries* and *agioi* of the Orthodox tradition, without forgetting our own sense of rhythm and ways of singing. A Latin American liturgy can only be ecumenical when it achieves this combination of the local and the global.

Some examples of ways of doing ecumenical liturgy in Brazil include a minimalist mass, eucharistic songs and "songs of the way".

Worshipping Together in the African Context

The "Village Meeting" Service

SAMUEL MWANIKI

This presentation took the form of a commentary on the liturgy of the "village meeting" (as printed below), a local annual interchurch worship event.

* * *

Gathering of the village

Call to worship

The village drums have sounded calling the people of God from our various villages in the north, south, east and west. We gather as one people, in the village of "All Hallows". *Ngai* (God) is among us. Let us sing, rejoice and dance. All who are thirsty come and drink of the living water. Come now and worship *Bwana* (Lord) our *Mungu* (God).

Song

Prayer of invocation

The village confession

Women: Our culture is thousands of years old,
ancient as the sun,
like the mountains of Kenya and Rwanda
and the Congo river of Zaire.

Men: We planted children and words.
We planted maize and yams.
We sang in the language of the drums of Africa.
We danced, dressed in the moonlight,
bedecked in the birds and the palms.
We were cultures in harmony with Mother nature.

The litany of confession was adapted from material from a women's conference (1992) of the Presbyterian Church, USA. The confession of faith is inspired by *The Gospel According to the Ghetto*, by Rev. Canaan Banana.

All: And, full of arrogance,
we destroyed it,
denying the identity of the peoples who are different.
All are part of the human family.

Women: We were at peace with ourselves
and with earth.

All: And we violated you
with the blade of the panga;
with flames of fire
we burned your tranquillity.

Men: We knew the gold of South Africa, the diamonds of Angola
and the silver of Zaire,
the noble woods of the forest of the Congo.
For us they were the holy ornaments on the body of mother earth.
We respected nature as we respected our own mother or father.

All: You gave us the beauty of the sea and its beaches,
You gave us earth and its secrets,
You gave us maize for our daily food,
the birds, the fishes, and the animal friends,
the fragrant fruits of the forest,
the soothing tea of eastern Africa,
the medicines of the earth became our nurse.

Men: And we plundered it,
denuding your forest,
cremating your fields
sowing poison in the rivers and in the air,
the generous earth.
Humanity against humanity.

Women: I was the free earth,
I was the clean water
I was the pure wind
fertile with abundance
full of songs.

All: And we divided you
with rules and borders.
With greed we destroyed the forest,
we lacerated the earth,
we invaded the fields,
we invaded humanity.

Silence

Retelling the story

Scripture reading

The village story-teller

Sermon

Song: Hallelujah

Affirmation of faith (the congregation stands)

I Believe

I believe in God, Mother Father spirit
who called the world into being,
who created men and women and set them free to live in love,
in obedience and community.

I believe in God, who because of love for the creation,
entered the world to share our humanity,
to rejoice and despair,
to set before us the paths of life and death;
to be rejected, to die, but finally
to conquer death and to bind the world to himself.

I believe in God who invites us into the community of the church
that we may, through faith and communion, experience
God's uplifting and sustaining grace;
that we may fulfil our human responsibility
and reach out for our neighbour;
that we may work to bring healing and wholeness
to a ruptured and uncertain world...
and that we may rejoice in the constancy of nature
and the joy of life itself.

I believe in God whose word teaches us
that the wheat and the tares grow together;
that the paths of life and death, good and evil,
too often converge...
choices are not clearly defined...
but we confidently and responsibly tread the path
we choose and only God can be our judge.

I believe in God who is present and working in this world
through men and women.

I sense God's purpose in a spark of light here and there
as humankind struggles to keep a human face.

I know God's purpose as I watch children at play...
hope born anew in each generation...
perhaps to be quickly extinguished,
perhaps to continue to burn brightly.

But for that hope I give thanks.

Sending forth

"Wa Wa Wa Emimimo"

The Church of South India Liturgy of the Eucharist

Authenticity and Relevance

SAMSON PRABHAKAR

Introduction

Since I became an ordained minister of the Church of South India and, later on, a member of an ecumenical community of the United Theological College, I have been searching for an answer to the question: in what way does the liturgy in which I participate express my faith as a Christian on the one hand, and as an Indian on the other? As the search continues, I am beginning to see the glimpses of my dual identities converging whenever I participate in the eucharistic liturgy of the Church of South India (CSI). I am also beginning to see more and more clearly that the CSI liturgy of the eucharist is authentically Christian and, to a certain extent, culturally relevant too. I also feel more strongly than ever that to be ecumenical, any Christian liturgy has to be authentically Christian and culturally relevant. Moreover, if our unity is to be visible, this is ultimately possible in and through fellowship at the Lord's table.

I have been asked to explore the use of liturgy within the united church's context and to address the questions: How does the worship within the CSI express and nurture the unity of this church? What liturgical problems has the church faced, and how has it resolved them? What problems remain unsolved? I will do this by drawing on my experience with the new CSI eucharistic liturgy.

This is a difficult task for a person like me who is neither an expert in the history of Christian worship nor a scholar in liturgical studies. But I take courage to stand before you from the fact that the liturgy committee which composed the eucharistic liturgy of the CSI consisted less of liturgical scholars than of persons whom someone is reported to have described as "for the most part liturgically illiterate".[1] Another member of the group confessed, "the liturgists might well have raised their eyebrows, had they taken the trouble to spy out our lack of credentials and training. However, what we lacked in knowledge, we made up for in enthusiasm."[2] When enthusiastic worshippers of God grapple together with a vision of visible unity through worship, the end result is something very beautiful and meaningful. So what emerged at the end was "a happy blend of contributions from the different heritages"[3] of all the denominations which had decided to join together as one church, the Church of South India.

The CSI eucharistic liturgy

Conscious of itself as a united church and desirous of expressing its unity visibly at the Lord's table, the CSI wondered what order of holy communion should be used. It was also mindful of the fact that the united church was a new chapter in ecumenical history and therefore should not allow itself to be dominated by any one of the constituent bodies, namely the Anglicans, Methodists, Congregationalists and Presbyterians.

> And so under pressure of this consciousness of a unity which transcended differences and of the general demand to which it gave expression, the executive committee of the synod asked the liturgy committee to prepare an order for the Lord's supper to be used in the first instance at the second synod which was to meet in January 1950.[4]

This liturgy was not published in printed form until 1962, and then with some minor modifications and additions.[5] However, it was well received by the members of the synod. Realizing that the use of the liturgy is a very sensitive issue and more a matter of the heart than the brain, and that it is the liturgy which promotes a sense of identity, the synod did not thrust it on the local congregations of the new-born church. Instead it allowed the congregations to continue to use their denominational liturgies.[6] But unexpectedly it received an enthusiastic welcome by most of the congregations. In this regard T.S. Garrett comments:

> Perhaps they have sensed that in using it they are claiming a richness in worship which was not always present in the tradition in which they were brought up. By so doing they are certainly not exchanging freedom for chains.[7]

The richness of the CSI liturgy is to be found in its faithful linkage to the roots of Christian tradition and its delicate linkage to the cultural heritage of India.

Authenticity

The mind of the liturgy committee which composed the liturgy of the eucharist may be evident in the statement made by the convener of the committee:

> It was felt unwise to attempt a mere expansion of any existing order of service, because the differences of usages and custom in our church are very great and no one tradition could satisfy everyone. We therefore tried to *base all our work* on that original apostolic tradition which we all accept and of which all our peculiar traditions are interpretations. We tried to base the liturgy, both in thought and as far as possible in its actual wording, on the scriptures themselves.[8]

Although various elements of the CSI eucharistic liturgy are now taken for granted and are common in many churches which use them in English as well as in four South Indian languages, a cursory look at the liturgy clearly shows how it is faithfully rooted in the soil of Judeo-Christian heritage.[9] Because of this, it is authentically Christian. And in being so it expresses the unity not only of the members of the CSI who gather together to break the bread, but also of those churches outside and within India that have originated from the same root. Regarding the authenticity of the CSI liturgy as a whole, E.C. Ratcliff comments as follows:

> The composers have produced rites, the meaning and content of which echo those of the ancient church... the new rites resemble the ancient in simplicity of pattern, logic of movement, the economy of prayer and ceremony.[10]

To be authentically Christian, a liturgy has to be ecumenical in its meaning, form and content. The CSI liturgy of the eucharist fulfils this as well. The fourth world conference on Faith and Order envisaged the following elements to be necessary for a eucharistic liturgy of an ecumenical community:

a) the service of the word containing: the reading and preaching of the word; intercession for the whole church and for the world;
b) a service of the sacrament, having a shape determined by the actions of our Lord at the last supper: taking bread and wine to be used by God in this service; blessing God for creation and redemption and invoking the Holy Spirit (or referring in some other way to the Holy Spirit); reciting the words of institution, whether before or within or after the prayer of thanksgiving and saying the Lord's prayer; breaking of the bread; giving the bread and wine.[11]

The CSI liturgy of the eucharist contains these and much more. It provides an opportunity for a devotion before the Lord's supper containing penitential matter like the decalogue and an exhortation, recommended for use on the night before and at an earlier time on the day of the communion.[12] Preparation for the eucharist consists of *Gloria in Excelsis* or the ancient hymn "Holy God...", a hymn of praise, a simple form of confession and absolution. The ministry of the word of God includes three readings from the Bible, a sermon, one of the two creeds and intercessions for the church and the world. The ministry of the sacrament includes its traditional fourfold pattern based on what the Lord did at the last supper, namely:

1) he took the bread and wine;
2) he blessed God over these gifts;
3) he broke the bread;
4) he gave the bread and wine to the disciples.

The fourfold pattern consists of ancient liturgical formulas, such as the *sursum corda*, the *sanctus*, and the Lord's Prayer. All these are indications of how the liturgy is grounded firmly on the Judeo-Christian heritage and nurtures the worshippers' identity as Christians. Besides the above elements, the most important element, namely the anamnesis, is also the traditional one, which according to Gibbard

> is... wisely restored with its recalling not only of the "precious death and passion" but also the "glorious resurrection and ascension" of our Lord. This balance has come from going back behind medievalism and the Reformation to the New Testament.[13]

The liturgy that was approved by the CSI synod in 1962 was revised in 1972 by the then liturgy committee.[14] A quick glance at the revised liturgy would show that there is hardly any change in the structure compared to the older one. The obvious changes in the content are: (1) the absence of the Nicene Creed; (b) the absence of the prayer called "prayer of humble access" just before the Lord's prayer and the actual breaking of the bread. The reasons for this obvious "censorship" are not known to me, though I tried to trace them by consulting two bishops of the CSI who were leaders at the time of revision. Besides these omissions, the revised edition has been made simpler in terms of language by doing away with archaic terminology and phrases in the liturgy that were rather difficult for the Indian celebrants. Apart from these changes, the revised edition seems to retain all the characteristics of the earlier one. As Anita Stauffer puts it:

> Our taproot is Jesus, and his death and resurrection, which itself is Jesus' new interpretation of the whole passover event — this is the most central core of the Christian faith, and it provides a pattern for everything we do, including our worship, the pattern for baptism and the pattern for eucharist. The test of authenticity is the gospel and the apostolic tradition, themselves patterned on Jesus the Christ.[15]

The liturgy of the CSI, in both the original and the revised form, is no exception to this.

Relevance

The relationship between the eucharist and the culture within which it is celebrated is an issue that has a bearing not only on the question of the worshippers' cultural rootedness and identity, but also on the question of unity. Unity is not uniformity. It is mutual respect and recognition. In the context of globalization, diversity of cultures has to be accepted as a reality — not as a threat to each other, but as an expression of God's creativity. Therefore, the issue is of ecumenical interest — not merely as a question of ecclesial unity but also one of the oneness of the human community. The authors of the eucharistic liturgy of the CSI seem to have been sensitive to this, but have not been able to make any progress in this regard (perhaps due to fear of syncretism). In general, liturgical forms in use in South India have mostly been imported from the West. Garrett says that even those elements which have had their birth in India show signs of Western influence.[16] The elements that are indigenous are the form of the greeting of peace, the silence and provision for extempore prayers.[17]

Even though the written liturgy of the eucharist is for the most part alien to Indian soil, we have used it in South India for 45 years. We have a faculty for assimilating foreign elements into our culture while still remaining Indian in essence. We still worship in church buildings that are mostly Gothic in architecture — but the worship offered in them is our own. "Somehow, an Indian atmosphere always succeeds in asserting itself."[18] In rural congregations of South India one can even now see worshippers seated on the floor, worshipping God by singing Indian music and using Indian and not Western musical instruments. These may be very superficial ways of being rooted in the culture of the soil, but still they are an important aspect of our expressing our kinship to our cultural heritage.

Once I was invited to celebrate the holy eucharist in a rural congregation near Bangalore. The congregation belongs to the CSI and has been using the CSI liturgy of the eucharist since it became a part of the church. To my pleasant surprise, all the congregational responses found in the liturgy, including the Lord's prayer and the creed, were sung by the congregation, not to Gregorian chant or an Anglican chant, but with a purely Indian tune, with an accompaniment of harmonium[19] and tabla.[20] Here I felt that the liturgy could be authentically Christian and culturally relevant without the fear of being syncretistic. Certainly we have a long way to go, but the signs of making the liturgy authentic and relevant are found here and there. Garrett had seen these signs already in the 1950s when he said:

> It is probably in such accessory elements of worship that the Indian spirit will continue to be most clearly manifest. In all the major Indian languages there has been Christian poetic creativity in the tradition of the great *bhakti* poets of Hinduism. The movement of preference for those "Christian lyrics", as they are called, is gaining ground, as against the translations of Western hymns which were at one time so popular (and in fact are still popular in urban, "elitist" congregations.) Indeed, India's Christian lyrical tradition may one day be discovered by the world as a classical contribution to literature.[21]

Here it must be pointed out that there are still some congregations in the CSI that continue to use their erstwhile denominational liturgies even after 45 years of "unity".

The efforts to express our cultural identity in and through the eucharistic liturgy are more clearly evident, not in our united church, but in other ecumenical institutions like the United Theological College, the Ecumenical Christian Centre, the National Christian Council, ashrams and so on.[22]

Conclusion

There are certainly other tensions than that between authenticity and relevance, but at the moment this seems to be the most crucial one within the CSI.[23] Since I have focused only on the liturgy of the eucharist, it may appear that in fact there is hardly anything "Indian" in the liturgy. That would be unfair because there are genuinely Indian elements in our worship material, such as a prayer based on the Upanishads in the liturgy of baptism, and the use of white garments and of a lamp. These are a point where "ancient Christian tradition and Indian religious sentiment meet".[24] Moreover, it has become widely accepted tradition in the CSI to use *tali* (originally a thread dipped in turmeric tied by the bridegroom around the neck of the bride and considered to be auspicious and sacred) at the marriage and also the "seven steps", both of which are genuinely Indian.

In conclusion, I am in full agreement with Tovey when he says:

> Clearly the Church of South India stands as a model of the relationship between liturgy and ecumenism. In the words of Ronald Jasper, "it marked a kind of watershed in the history of liturgical revision; it coloured the thinking of would-be revisers; and its influence, whether direct or indirect, was undeniable".[25]

NOTES

[1] T.S. Garrett, *Worship in the Church of South India*, London, Lutterworth, 1958, p.12.
[2] *Ibid.*, p.13.
[3] *Ibid.*, p.8.
[4] *Ibid.*, p.13.
[5] Please see the CSI document "Eucharist: Ecumenical Convergence", column 1, for the text of the CSI liturgy, 1962.
[6] "Every pastor and congregation shall have freedom to determine the forms of their public worship." CSI Constitution, chapter 10, p.59.
[7] Garrett, *op. cit.*, p.8.
[8] As cited by Mark S. Gibbard, "Liturgical Life in the Church of South India", *Studia Liturgica*, vol. 3, no. 4, 1964, pp.195-96.
[9] The tendency to take the liturgical elements for granted is mainly due to two reasons: (1) there is a dearth of literature on the CSI liturgy written by Indian worshippers for the use of the common people as well as theologians, and (2) the primary function of the new liturgy appears to be to unite the fragmented Christianity which is a minority community.
[10] As cited by Philip Tovey, "Liturgy and Ecumenism: Three Models of Development", in *Liturgy in Dialogue*, eds Paul Bradshaw & Bryan Spinks, London, SPCK, 1993, p.70.
[11] *The Fourth World Conference on Faith and Order: The Report From Montreal 1963*, eds P.C. Rodger & L. Vischer, Faith and Order paper no. 42, London, SCM, 1964, p.74.
[12] The document entitled "Eucharist: Ecumenical Convergence" does not include this material for the simple reason that, to the best of my knowledge, no one uses it. However, the material is adapted from the Basle Mission liturgy.
[13] Gibbard, *op. cit.*, p.198.
[14] Please see the CSI document "Eucharist: Ecumenical Convergence", column 2.
[15] "Christian Worship: Toward Localization and Globalization", *Worship and Culture in Dialogue*, ed. S. Anita Stauffer, LWF Studies, Geneva, Lutheran World Federation, 1994, p.11.
[16] Garrett, *op. cit.*, pp.8-9.
[17] Shaking hands with both the palms or hand clasping. Silent meditation is a typically Indian way of speaking to God.
[18] Garrett, *op. cit.*, p.9.
[19] The harmonium is an Indian version of a miniature organ, normally used to accompany the singers and assist them to maintain the musical line and correct harmonies.

[20] A percussion instrument consisting of two drums.
[21] Garrett, *op. cit.*, p.9.
[22] What Tovey, *op. cit.*, describes in the section "interchurch bodies" applies in these instances.
[23] Other tensions are mentioned by Stauffer, *op. cit.*, pp.13-15.
[24] As cited by Tovey, *op. cit.*, p.71.
[25] *Ibid.*

BIBLIOGRAPHY

Avila, Raphael, *Worship and Politics*, Maryknoll, NY, Orbis, 1981.

Baptism, Eucharist and Ministry 1982-1990: Report on the Process and Responses, Faith and Order Paper no. 149, Geneva, WCC, 1990.

Bergsma, Joop, "The Eucharistic Prayer in Non-Roman Catholic Churches of the West Today", in *Studia Liturgica*, vol. 11, nos 3 & 4, 1976, pp.177-205.

Best, Thomas F., ed., *Living Today towards Visible Unity: The Fifth International Consultation of United and Uniting Churches*, Faith and Order paper no. 142, Geneva, WCC, 1988.

Best, Thomas F., ed., *Faith and Order 1985-1989*, Faith and Order paper no. 148, Geneva, WCC, 1990.

Burki, Bruno, "The Lima Text as a Standard for Current Understanding and Practice of the Eucharist", in *Studia Liturgica*, vol. 16, nos 1 & 2, pp.64-77.

Chupungco, Anscar, "The Lima Text as a Pointer to the Future: An Asian Perspective", in *Studia Liturgica*, vol. 16, nos 1 & 2, 1986, pp.100-107.

Davies, J.G., ed., *A New Dictionary of Liturgy and Worship*, London, SCM, 1986.

Garrett, T.S., *Worship in the Church of South India*, London, Lutterworth, 1958.

Gibbard, Mark S., "Liturgical Life in the Church of South India", *Studia Liturgica*, vol. III, no. 4, 1964.

Lanne, Emmanuel, "The Lima Text: A Contribution to the Unity of the Churches", in *Studia Liturgica*, vol. 16, nos 1 & 2, 1986, pp.108-127.

Lott, E.J., ed., *Worship in an Indian Context*, Bangalore, United Theological College, 1986.

Prabhakar, S., ed., *A Celebration of Hope*, NCCI, India, 1991.

Stauffer, Anita S., "Christian Worship: Toward Localization and Globalization", in *Worship and Culture in Dialogue*, ed. S. Anita Stauffer, LWF Studies, Geneva, Lutheran World Federation, Geneva, 1994.

Tovey, Philip, "Liturgy and Ecumenism", in *Liturgy in Dialogue*, eds Paul Bradshaw & B. Spinks, London, SPCK, 1993.

Vischer, Lukas, "The Epiclesis: Sign of Unity and Renewal", in *Studia Liturgica*, vol. 6, no. 1, 1969, pp.30-39.

Wainwright, Geoffrey, "The Eucharist as an Ecumenical Sacrament of Reconciliation and Renewal", in *Studia Liturgica*, vol. 11, no. 1, 1976, pp.1-17.

Some Experiences of Orthodoxy in the Search for "Koinonia"

SOPHIE DEICHA

The Ecumenical Patriarchate of Constantinople was among the first to see the need for seeking the road towards Christian unity. The Orthodox call, issued in 1920 in a letter addressed to all the churches inviting them to form a "koinonia", bore fruit both in Europe as well as in the rest of the world. The European Parliament was reminded of this invitation in a speech by the Ecumenical Patriarch during his visit in April 1994.[1] In the search for ecumenism in Europe today, the meaning of "koinonia" is more important than ever.

If such a strong conviction of the need for an ecumenical "koinonia" could develop within Orthodoxy, it is the result largely of its liturgical experience.[2] The Orthodox vision of unity is a global one: it does not separate theology, worship and life. This was made clear by Orthodox theologians in Western Europe. Archpriest Sergius Boulgakov (1871-1944), the half-centenary of whose death we now remember,[3] insisted on the importance of both prayer and worship from the beginnings of Faith and Order, as well as the place which must be given in the liturgy to those who themselves have born faithful witness in their own lives.[4]

At a meeting last July in Lisieux, organized by one of the oldest ecumenical associations in France ("Amitié" — A meeting among Christians) which has been coming together since 1927, I had a particularly moving liturgical experience. In the context of meetings devoted to the general theme of inculturation, regular times were allotted to liturgical prayer. The Catholic and Protestant leaders interpolated something new and quite unexpected into the usual cycle of confessional and "ecumenical" liturgies: this was to "name", in the context of prayer, the "heros" of the faith from the very simple to the most illustrious bishop/evangelist.[5] Suddenly I became aware of an Orthodox "presence", the witness of human beings bearing within themselves the church.

At this event, we revived an ancient liturgical tradition attested to since the earliest centuries of the church. "Koinonia" reveals itself in all the diversity of life when its concrete dimensions enter our liturgical memory through personal experience.[6] The recognition in the liturgical assembly of this human witness is an ecclesial act which becomes one of the expressions of "koinonia" between local churches.

This text has been translated from the French by Canon Prof. David Holeton, and the notes by the WCC Language Service.

The fullness of ecclesial communion is expressed in the *communio sanctorum* in its most complete sense. At the first meeting of Faith and Order in Lausanne in 1927, this liturgical question was posed by the Orthodox participants. Since then, it has not lost its importance as was made clear at the Stuttgart meeting of the Standing Commission in 1993.[7]

Similarly, the place occupied by holy icons in worship also expresses this reality of "koinonia". Icons are a witness that the human being, called to live in Christ and the Holy Spirit, is to become a participant in the divine nature.[8] Today, icons are coming to occupy an increasingly important place in the life of prayer of Christians of all denominations.

While there is as yet no systematic liturgical study of the icon, I would like to underline its importance as one path towards a synthesis that does not separate faith, prayer and life.[9] The explicit invocation of the saints in an ecumenical context is still done only rarely. But an approach to ethics from the point of view of "koinonia" or "hagio-ethics" was part of the discussions of the European Ecumenical Assembly at Basel in 1989,[10] and the role of icons played an important part.

The example of the solemn celebration on 4 August 1993 in the cathedral of St James in Compostela, to mark the opening of the fifth world conference on Faith and Order, is important. In the processions, each of which carried a cross, an icon, and an evangelary, it became clear that icons did not have a merely decorative character, but a liturgical one also.[11] During the conference, at the ecumenical service on the Feast of the Transfiguration, the icon of the Transfiguration was given its proper place with the other icons on the iconostasis where it remained for the whole day.[12] The silent presence of the icons certainly heightened the prayer of the assembly and its sense of "koinonia".

It would be interesting to bring together the explanations of icons from an ecumenical point of view. Let us take the example of the tenth assembly of the Conference of European Churches in Prague in 1992. There, Roublev's icon of the angelic visitors (often called the icon of the Trinity), often the first to be discovered ecumenically by those who do not know icons, was one of the elements used to nourish the assembly's meditation on the theme of "koinonia".[13]

The richness of the dogmatic content of icons illustrates that in Orthodoxy "the development of dogma is not distinct from liturgical life" and therefore retains its doxological character:

> Given that dogma... is principally limited to the praise of Christ and the Trinity and has kept its place in liturgical life, the Orthodox church is basically freer in resolving new theological problems.[14]

Icons also play an important role in the question of inculturation and ecclesialization.[15] This ability to integrate cultural, social, artistic, scientific and other work is beginning to be recognized in the ecumenical movement.[16] New modalities need to be discovered here in order to find a holistic approach. What Orthodoxy has to bring to this discussion is not without importance. "Koinonia" is realized through persons in communion — their imperfections notwithstanding. For those who are not familiar with icons, particularly those of the saints and the witness they bear to the presence of God at the very heart of daily life, this may be less than convincing.

> But does God not reveal himself through the cross, the supreme "failure"? It is precisely through this "failure" that both theology and the icon bear their witness to God and make

> present the divine presence — that presence which, in its reality, is accessible in the experience of holiness.[17]

After my experience in July at Lisieux and those of recent ecumenical assemblies, it seems to me that the time has come to raise the question of the importance of the human life experience — particularly that of the saints — both for the liturgy and for our common search for "koinonia".

There have been many achievements in the past sixty years of ecumenical liturgical research in Western Europe. They certainly cannot all be listed here. I will relegate the Orthodox contributions to that search, and to the beginnings of Faith and Order, to a footnote and rather raise a question about the current situation.[18]

It is said that by the year 2000, half the population of Europe will be Orthodox. Such demographic changes demand our attention. It will become increasingly important to craft our ecumenical liturgical prayer in a shape that will be more recognizable to our sisters and brothers who are neophytes in ecumenical dialogue and less adept at it than were their ecumenical forbears from the Orthodox diaspora. Those who will be entering ecumenical dialogue for the first time will be looking for signs which they recognize from their own liturgical life.

It is the Holy Spirit that draws us into "koinonia" both with one another and in the intimacy of the life of the Trinity: "Those who love me will keep my word, and my Father will love them, and we will come to them and make our home with them" (John 14:23). Liturgical celebrations in ecumenical assemblies can deepen this experience of "koinonia" and help us to rediscover the human element which is within them.

NOTES

[1] Speech by His Holiness the Ecumenical Patriarch Bartholomew before the assembly of the European Parliament in Strasbourg on 19 April 1994: "Whenever, in the ecumenical unity of the churches, we have dared 'according to our strength' or even 'beyond our strength' we have benefitted because of our weakness and not because of our strength. In 1920 the Ecumenical Patriarch took the initiative, in an encyclical letter, of inviting the Christian churches and confessions to form a 'League of Churches'... That initiative, together with the efforts of the Protestant confessions, gave birth to the World Council of Churches. There, despite the existing weaknesses, a fruitful exchange has developed among the traditions, with a common philanthropy and the building of mutual respect for differences in the shaping of consciences."

[2] The Orthodox approach, conscious of the difficulties, is also familiar with the presence and action of Christ and the Holy Spirit in the eucharistic assembly and in the personal daily life of the faithful. Prayer, continuing from generation to generation, gives the inner assurance that antinomies such as unity and division can be resolved by the "koinonia of the Holy Spirit". By way of example, here are two prayers from the beginning and the end of the eucharistic liturgy: "For the peace of the whole world, for the stability of the holy churches of God, and for the union of all, let us pray to the Lord." "Having asked for the unity of the Faith, and the communion of the Holy Spirit..."

[3] In memory of Father Sergius Bulgakov, "Proclaiming the Gospel in Present-day Cultures", a lecture given at Lisieux on 12 July 1994.

[4] "Approach to the Mystery of the Church in the Homilies of Father Sergius Bulgakov", opening lecture at the symposium to mark the 50th anniversary of the death of Bulgakov, Regensburg, 5-10 August 1994. Besides his prayers for unity, he has also left a series of ecumenical homilies. We have stressed the importance of these for the approach to "koinonia" in a Trinitarian perspective. His other writings of an ecumenical nature are more widely known.

[5] St Cyril and St Methodius (IX c), St Stephen of Perm (1340-96), St Tryphon of Pechenegs (1583), St Gouri, Bishop of Kazan, St Germain of Alaska (1757-1836), Pierre l'Aléoute, St Innocent of Moscow (1797-1879), St Nicolas of Japan, Equal of the Apostles (1836-1912).

[6] S. Deicha, *Cours d'Hagiologie*, Paris, St Sergius Institute of Orthodox Theology, 1993.

[7] *Minutes of the Meeting of the Faith and Order Standing Commission 1993*, Stuttgart, Germany, Faith and Order Paper no. 165, p.52.

[8] 2 Peter 1:4.

[9] "Iconographie et hagiologie", in *Istina*, 1988, no. 1.

[10] European Ecumenical Assembly (15-21 May 1989), Geneva, Conference of European Churches, 1989, p.125; "La foi que nous affirmons", in *Unité des chrétiens*, 1990, no. 77; see also "Heiligenverehrung", in *Orthodoxes Forum: Zeitschrift des Instituts für Orthodoxe Theologie der Universität München*, 1992, Heft 1.

[11] Cf. *Oros* of the Ecumenical Council of Nicea II.

[12] On the significance of this feast for the theme of "koinonia", see the worship book of the fifth world conference on Faith and Order, Santiago de Compostela, 1993, WCC, Geneva, pp.x-xi.

[13] "It needs an artist like the painter of the Rublev icon to capture something of the divine reality of 'koinonia' for us. Or a poet like the author of St John's Gospel." Paper by Mary Tanner, delivered 2 September 1992, in *God Unites – In Christ a New Creation*, report of the tenth assembly of the Conference of European Churches, 1-11 September 1992, Prague, Geneva, CEC, 1993, p.99.

[14] "The Significance of the Orthodox Church for the Ecumenical Movement", E. Schlink, *Theologia*, Athens, 1973 (in German).

[15] "A people does not just passively receive the church's pictorial language. Rather, it does so creatively by introducing local artistic traditions into it. It blossoms according to its own character, in regard both to holiness and the outward expression of it — sacred art. The unity of the faith and the sacraments causes this variety because it includes a constantly new and vital experience of Tradition, which is necessarily original and creative." In L. Ouspensky, *La théologie de l'icône*, Paris, Cerf, 1982.

[16] "Le concept de nature", closing lecture at the fifth European Conference on Science and Theology, Freising, Munich, 27 March 1994.

[17] *La théologie de l'icône*, *op. cit.*, p.463.

[18] As we have seen, Fr Bulgakov was the first to reflect on these questions in the light of his experience in Faith and Order. While he agreed with what he called "confessional ascesis", he was nonetheless irritated. He found it intolerable to be obliged to say nothing on such important questions as the *communio sanctorum* in worship. He therefore tried to express the difficulties he encountered in the form of antinomies, not in order to brush them aside but in the hope that they could be resolved: on the one hand, the inner need to affirm the Orthodox faith in the fullness of the liturgy; and on the other, the awareness of a process of compromise in which it almost seemed that out of kindness or friendship, some of that fullness had to be relinquished.

The solution would be given, as he wrote in *Près du puits de Jacob* ("By Jacob's Well"): "The Holy Spirit, the grace of the Holy Spirit can indeed resolve this antinomy into a new synthesis — not through agreements or compromises, but through a new inspiration... when we raise our eyes to heaven, then earthly boundaries cease to exist."

But he revised his idea. Did not barriers still persist in moments dedicated to prayer? He attached great importance to the place of prayer in the work of Faith and Order: "Spiritual life... in the meetings of representatives of different confessions enables us to get to know one another... it is more effective than words, it unites us and places us before our responsibilities... without this experience there can be no Christian unity. This unification in Christ, through the kinship of Christian experience, is a sort of sacrament of spiritual life."

While this new inspiration could, according to Fr Bulgakov, be based on the common heritage of the first millennium, the limitations to koinonia had been imposed unilaterally, without any justification. To accept them amounted to curtailing a whole dimension of koinonia in worship, namely, that which is linked to witness in its most concrete form, the recognition of the human being in his/her vocation to holiness. This, then, was one of the first questions concerning ecumenical worship raised by the Orthodox of the diaspora in Western Europe in the twenties and thirties.

Worship in United Congregations

HUGH CROSS

Introduction

Local ecumenical partnerships (LEPs for short) have been part of the English church scene since the mid-1960s, and can be found in a growing number of other countries, notably Aotearoa-New Zealand where the next highest concentration occurs.

They appear in three kinds. One is where local Christians originating from two or more traditions share fully in congregational life, interchange of ordained ministry, and shared eucharistic worship. The second is found where two or more congregations from different traditions share a building for worship and other uses. The third is known as a local covenant, in which two or more local congregations in a neighbourhood or village covenant for mission together, while retaining their individual lifestyles, buildings, worship and ministry.

In this paper I limit myself to giving indications about the first, the united congregation of two or more traditions. I shall also concentrate on eucharistic worship because it is the area where most interchurch difficulties occur in worship, and where LEPs have found that unity is possible. I do not have many texts to offer as samples, and what I have to say will explain why.

My paper tries to cover (a) what LEPs have learned through their experience and understanding of worship in the search for unity, (b) the problems encountered and their resolution, and (c) unresolved problems.

LEP learning through experience

Let me tell you a story. In 1969 an Anglican priest and I, a Baptist minister, were appointed to pioneer and develop united church mission on a new and growing housing development in the south-east of England. About 120 new homes had been built in an area that today has about 3000. We were instructed by our sending churches to develop a united project which would engage in mission during the week, and at weekends people would be expected to attend their several denominational churches elsewhere in the town. It was an impossible task because the first lesson we learnt was that Christians who mission together will seek to worship together, especially if they live in the same community and their task is to build community. The people whom we served in that community very quickly wanted us to arrange Sunday worship for them together. So, does unity achieved produce common worship, or does united worship build unity?

In those heady days of the late 1960s and early 1970s many of us engaged in developing new united congregations took the view that new wine needed new wine-skins, and we asked ourselves what united worship might look like when all the churches were united. In our own congregation we began with the revised Methodist Sunday service which had just been produced. The Church of England was then producing experimental liturgies known as "Series 2", and later "Series 3" services, among them the eucharist. So everything was in flux liturgically. We produced a liturgy suitable for our congregational needs based on the Methodist and Anglican Series 2 forms. Annually we held a congregational meeting intended to amend or revise or confirm what we were doing. Here we found that the second lesson to be learned was that united worship challenges people to rethink their own theology, to move out from habitual and unexamined practices, and to undertake the exciting or daunting task of coming to terms with new practices and thoughts on worship.

With that lesson we learnt another, namely, and obviously, that united worship broadens the worship experience of the participants, and sometimes leaves them feeling unsatisfied when engaging in their own narrowly-denominational liturgies and practices elsewhere.

There were other things happening, too. We were a company of human beings drawn together from a variety of experiences and pilgrimages. New folk joined us, bringing their own histories and experience and expectations. Each addition challenged us to listen to what people said, and to adapt or dialogue. Some folk were critical, some were wildly enthusiastic, and all of us found we were being confronted by changes, some of which we liked, and some we found difficult. But we all accepted changes and new experiences because we found a new breadth of belonging and a new sense of Christian oneness, which was greater than our divisions and our likes and dislikes. That was our fourth lesson.

In another LEP the participants argued that to adopt one of their denominational liturgies could be exclusive and divisive. They looked around for a liturgy that had already been tested in an ecumenical context, and came upon that of the Church of South India. The CSI had been born out of the same denominational traditions which were represented in the new LEP. So they took the CSI eucharist and adapted it for their own context; they use it still, fifteen or more years on.

Other LEPs took the view that it was important for people to be able to share in worship that was recognizable as far as their own experience of denominational worship was concerned. They were also concerned lest they should spawn a new denomination that would cut people off from their heritage. So they chose to have a cycle of denominational liturgies. Not only did this root people in their own traditions while engaging ecumenically, but also it exposed them to the liturgies of other Christians, making it possible for them to visit or move to churches of other denominations without feeling uncomfortable with a different liturgical experience. However, the lesson to be learnt from this practice is that it can lead to the LEP using liturgies which have become redundant in their denominational context, and so defeating the object.

That fact — that denominational liturgies have been evolving over these past thirty years — also had a part to play in LEP experience and learning. There has been a convergence of liturgies, so that today many of them are easily accepted and understood by cross-denominational worshippers. In the past twelve or so years, too,

Baptism, Eucharist and Ministry has been a uniting factor in eucharistic worship. Indeed, some LEPs use the Lima liturgy as one of the options for Sunday use. In one LEP where I have been officiating regularly recently, Lima is preferred because its language (as adapted locally) is more inclusive than either the Anglican rite or the Methodist rite.

Since the earliest days of LEPs it has been a rule that any liturgy planned for regular use in a LEP must be submitted to the sponsoring body, the meeting of denominational representatives providing episkope for the project. Sometimes this has allowed great flexibility and experiment, and sometimes it has applied a more rigorous examination of texts. I think it is true to say that now the position has been reached where there is much less experimentation in eucharistic worship in LEPs than there was, and, as I have shown, this is partly the result of liturgical developments in the denominations involved.

Problems

Not so much a problem as a dilemma is the fact that every LEP has to face the question whether or not what it is doing is making a new denomination. If the project retains denominational rites, it can be said to be demonstrating that the churches can worship together comfortably, while still retaining their own denominational identities. On the other hand, if the project develops a new rite for its own use it can be said to be demonstrating that Christians from several traditions can, with a bit of flexibility, become truly united and develop a liturgy that expresses that unity.

Again, not so much a problem as a hurdle to jump is the fact that each tradition has its own rules which it expects the LEP to keep. Where Roman Catholics are partners in any project, of course, there can be no sharing of the eucharist. Some traditions require that only an ordained minister may preside at the eucharist, while others provide for a "properly authorized" person to do so. Some require the use of fermented wine, while others expressly forbid it. Some expect that the remaining elements be consumed, while others allow them to be disposed of as seems best. None of these is a matter which cannot be dealt with by careful dialogue and sensitive practice. They become insuperable only where an inflexible approach is taken, and where there is an unwillingness to hear the points of view of others.

Take the matter of fermented or unfermented wine, for instance. In some LEPs fermented wine is presented in the chalice, while unfermented wine is offered in the "thimbles" common in free churches.

Unresolved problems

As I reflect upon the subject I have come to the conclusion that what the LEPs tell us is that all things are possible, given trust and the willingness to learn. The one major problem which has so far not been resolved satisfactorily is that of lay presidency at communion. In other words the stumbling block is not the eucharist but ministry.

The issue is, in what does ordination consist? In a tradition where the congregation is the highest authority, it could be argued that a person duly called and tested by the church meeting and authorized to preside at the Lord's table might be understood to be ordained. A church which recognizes the right of another church to ordain whomsoever it wishes could well be expected to accept that the decision of church meeting might be said to be all the authority required. Given that that position is taken, however, a tension then occurs where there is a partnership between a congregationally ordered church and a presbyterian or episcopal church. Let me illustrate this with an actual example from Milton Keynes, where I now work. After much thought the sponsoring body has approved rules which will allow lay presidency in one of the ecumenical parishes. However, Methodist local preachers and Anglican lay ministers are not permitted to preside because in their own denominational context they would not be allowed to do so. The compromise has been brokered, but it includes the prospect of hurt for some in being excluded from what they see as an option for them.

"Saying What We Mean and Meaning What We Say"

RODNEY MATTHEWS

Liturgy: a paradigm for ecumenism

It has occurred to me in preparing for this consultation that sound liturgy is itself in some ways a paradigm of the ecumenical movement and our search for unity. What I mean is this. In all good liturgy there is a recognizable framework, a "given", into which is poured a rich variety of content in response to God's dialogue with us and our search to know him. Furthermore, this experience of worship itself thrusts us back out into the world from which we have come seeking to know the mind of God, and engages us in the *missio Dei*. All is within the pattern of God, who gives us freedom to explore but the discipline of commitment. He calls us to say what we mean and to mean what we say.

Certainly the liturgical paradigm is true of the covenant in Wales about which I have been invited to speak to you or, as I prefer to express it, to paint a picture of many colours, all complementing one another within the pattern of a *rainbow*. ENFYS is the Welsh word for "rainbow", expressing the covenant entered into nearly twenty years ago by five denominations in Wales, one episcopal and four "free" churches — although the Anglican church in Wales is itself a free church, becoming disestablished in 1920.

The text of the covenant (1974)

You have before you (see p.94 below) the text of that covenant committing us to

> work and pray in common obedience to our Lord Jesus Christ, in order that by the Holy Spirit we may be brought into ONE VISIBLE CHURCH to serve together in mission to the glory of God the Father.

The *missio Dei*. You will quickly notice that the clauses of the covenant follow a pattern which provides, if you like, a liturgical framework for our self-expression and mutual discovery in our dialogue with each other and with God.

My task is to paint some finer lines on a broad canvas, so that you can see how many Christians in Wales are learning that we are all one in Christ, in the faith, mission, apostolicity, membership, worship and authority: a sound framework for exploration, experiment and expression, all good aspects of worship.

The pattern of reports and services

I will be referring to a number of reports and liturgical texts, which are printed (or sometimes summarized or commented upon) at the end of my paper.

I am bound to declare a particular interest in the material I present. I have to own up to dipping a paintbrush in the palette over the past 18 years and helping to paint the picture you will now see. I also like to think that I am actually in the picture, a self-portrait if you like, as I *use* this material, trying week by week among the people to whom I minister to ensure that we say what we mean and mean what we say. But lest too vivid an imagination carry me away a senior churchman sounds a note of caution. "These covenanting publications", wrote the Rt Rev. Cledan Mears, formerly Bishop of Bangor, last month concerning the latest liturgical text from Wales,

> contain material that is streets ahead of the ecumenical movement at the local and national level, but they are there as a challenge to the churches to shake themselves from their indolence and indifference, a disease that will prove mortal unless they do.

In that considered judgment lies a double warning but also a fulsome promise. The warning is that liturgists should not live in ivory towers and their ideas must always be earthed in living situations; at the same time those living situations need the food of ecumenical imagination or they will wither. What promise there is, therefore, in what I will try to share with you lies in the way in which the *principle* of unity is being put into *practice* in Wales.

The covenant in principle

First some broad brush strokes to suggest the outline of the picture, against which background I will attempt some finer points of colourful detail. In our covenant there is mutual recognition and common intention.

The *recognition* is that we see in each other marks of the true church with regard to those fundamentals I mentioned earlier: faith, mission, apostolicity, membership, ministry, worship and authority. The *intention* is that in all these areas of realized unity or actual brokenness we may seek to bring ourselves nearer to one another so that Christ can make us whole together.

"Principles of visible unity in Wales" (1980)

That, then, is the canvas on which our picture is painted and the outline in sketch form. The first task in filling it in was perhaps the easiest because it remained academic: it was to produce in 1980 what we called "Principles of Visible Unity in Wales" (see p.95 below), a study in what would be required in exploring these great themes.

The obvious and significant starting point was worship. If Christians cannot worship together they are unlikely to be able to do much else together and what they do apart may have a hollow ring. From the outset we were optimistic. As the 1980 report said:

> In the course of time the uniting church can be expected to evolve its own distinctive approach to worship, expressed in totally new patterns and liturgical forms.

There was a reason for this. From the earliest days when we tried to come together for eucharistic worship, which we judged to be pivotal — a means to unity as well as its goal, an expression of unity already realized — we discovered that the only rite readily available in which all could join in full conscience was that of the Church of South India.

But it was an intrusion into *our* picture, a foreign style, coming from a different culture and — even for the Welsh — curiously long and "wordy"! In short, it was not really "us" and we believed not so much that we could improve on it but rather that much would be gained by painting our own liturgy. It was not that we were going to eschew Christian tradition down through the ages; on the contrary, we are committed to unity which preserves continuity with all God's people so far as we are able to discover and achieve.

"The holy communion" (1981) (see p.96 below)

It is for that reason that "The Holy Communion: [the Rite of the] Covenanted Churches in Wales" appears to some to be a close sister of the Church of England's 1980 Alternative Service Book Rite A, and to others to be very like the English text of the Roman Catholic Mass. But those who know the Celtic history of Wales will readily appreciate that the last thing we would do would be to follow slavishly either Canterbury or Rome.

What we set out to do was to produce a rite that was indigenous to the Welsh covenant with an economy of words, elements that would challenge one another as innovative, whilst marrying continuity with our contemporary mission.

The first intention of this covenanted rite was to provide an agreed text for occasions of joint eucharistic worship. Beyond that it was up to any church to use or adapt it through whatever means was within its own authority. The results have exceeded our expectations, although there remain some disappointments. Its use has been wider than we at first envisaged and has gone far beyond Wales. In some places it is now the recognized form of a weekly communion service. In other churches, such as the Baptist church of which I am minister, it provides a framework for our weekly liturgy within which there are many variations.

"The Holy Communion: Supplement" (1993) (see p.96 below)

Incidentally, it was always intended that it should be used as flexibly as possible within a clear liturgical framework, and when we found that too often it was becoming a new straitjacket, we produced a supplement to encourage liberation. The service itself has become the basis on which we have produced further texts to which I will come in a moment.

One disappointment to me personally over this communion rite will illustrate how difficult it is to encourage people out of unnecessary ruts. I argued strongly to include within the rubrics the recommendation that where possible both a common loaf *and* a common cup be used. This was not only for the most obvious symbolic reasons but also because — I thought — by that single stroke two different aberrations from tradition would be challenged.

In some places, including my own church, that goal has been achieved as it is in most local ecumenical partnerships. But more often, especially on occasions of united services, what tends to happen is that "the tradition" of the host church is maintained: thus sometimes it is a common cup but individual wafers; and sometimes a common loaf but individual communion glasses. Is that too subtle a point to worry about? I think it represents a problem of stunted growth which we have yet to overcome.

"Ministry in a Uniting Church" (1986) (see p.101 below)

Indeed, as we come to the next exercise we undertook, that of the massive challenge of edging our respective ordained ministries from recognition to reconciliation in a report entitled "Ministry in a Uniting Church", this very blinkered view of ecumenism (that all that needs to happen is for everyone to fall in with us and do things our way) was specifically challenged. I quote from the introduction:

> The churches must resist the temptation to see the uniting church of the future as their own denomination writ large and to ask other churches to change in order to fit in with their present self-understanding and pattern. Instead each must ask of itself: How can we be renewed and changed in order to receive God's gift of unity?

It is beyond the scope of this particular consultation to go into the detail of how we tackled the vexed questions of ministry. (Suffice it to say that the responses to our 1986 report were so complex that some misjudged them as rejections of it. They were not and we are even now, eight years on, probing the next exciting possibilities of episcope because this was one of the surprisingly positive things to emerge — that non-episcopal churches may be ready to move this log-jam.)

What may be of more immediate interest in the context of this consultation on *liturgy*, however, was one discovery we made almost by accident during our theological debates on how to reconcile existing ministries.

In a nutshell, or perhaps a cameo picture in the total landscape, it is this. As we struggled to express what would be necessary (and unnecessary) with regard to reconciliation, we realized — somewhat late in the day when the churches were calling for our report — that certain theological truths can best be expressed in liturgical form. *We can say what we mean and we can mean what we say*. The best we could offer at that stage was a sequel to our report as soon as we could we could manage it.

"The Inauguration of a Uniting Church in Wales: Draft Services" (1987) (see p.101 below)

Once again I must admit disappointment that by the time our supplementary document was published the following year too many people had already *misunderstood* what was in the main text and argued against it from a false premise. If they had waited the picture might have been different.

In the introduction to "The Inauguration of a United Church in Wales: Draft Services" we wrote: "It has long been recognized that the clearest expression of what Christians believe is to be found in the way they worship." We went on to demonstrate in the liturgical text that followed exactly what was involved in the mutual laying on of hands that meant that *no* minister was being re-ordained but that *all* ministers were having the limits of their existing ministry extended:

> May God continue his blessing already given in your ordination; may he use our action here for the reconciliation of all our ministries within the uniting church in Wales.

We proposed that we should say what we meant and mean what we said. No theoretical report could have expressed it more clearly than would be demonstrated in the act of worship. I believe that one day, and I pray for it to be sooner rather than later, when we are ready to inaugurate a uniting church in Wales, that draft liturgy will be the bones on which flesh will be seen and the breath of God breathed afresh into the valleys of Wales.

"Christian Baptism and Church Membership: A Rite of Baptism for the Covenanted Churches and an Essay on Baptism and Membership" (Parts 1 & 2) (1990) **(see p.103 below)**

But we are not sitting idly waiting for that day to come. Even while the churches were considering these questions of ministry we took on board a further study on membership. Once again it has had a necessary liturgical thrust: namely, concerning baptism and, for want of an alternative word for the present, confirmation.

How can churches be united when it seems that the theology of baptism divides them? (Remember, nineteen years into the covenant I am still called "a Baptist" as a mark of particular distinction.)

We tried now to marry two methods of covenanting progress. With "The Holy Communion: [The Rite of the] Covenanted Churches in Wales" text, churches had a practical tool, a means to express and experiment. With the report "Ministry in a Uniting Church" they had a theological essay to examine and evaluate. Now we purposed to produce in one and the same process both experimental material *and* theological evaluation.

Thus what we argued in "Christian Baptism and Church Membership" was that baptism into the body of Christ is *one*. It *must* unite. It cannot divide and be authentic. "There is one Lord, one faith, *one* baptism." We must therefore find a way of *expressing* this fundamental unity liturgically if we are to "say what we mean and mean what we say". The first part of that report, therefore, contained an experimental rite of baptism, one service reflecting both the baptism of believers and the baptism of infants.

The theological and liturgical point is this. If you have two different texts, one for believers and one for infants, it is very difficult to maintain that baptism is *one*. But if there is a common liturgy — and if on occasion there might even be in the same service both believers *and* infants to be baptized — then the unity of baptism will become apparent. It was not easy to produce a text that was authentic to both cases, and only time will tell whether we have succeeded. But you will see as you examine this text that the only variation between the two is that in the case of the baptism of an infant a simple additional statement makes clear what is happening in a way that is self-apparent in the baptism of a believer and therefore does not need saying again.

Once again this rite is set in the context of "The Holy Communion" liturgy. It has been accepted for experimental use by all the covenanted churches as an alternative to their rites, especially where a candidate for believers' baptism is sensitive to the quest for unity and requests this, or where the parents of a child are from two different church traditions, or in local ecumenical partnerships.

If, in the course of time, it becomes the favoured rite for all our churches even before a united church is inaugurated, it will help to show that baptism is not into a denomination but into the church. (How many times have you heard someone say, "I was baptized a Methodist", as if that is the fundamental point?)

Here is a further point argued in the accompanying essay. It is Christian baptism that signifies entry into the church, the body of Christ. Nothing more is needed to put any seal on that status of church membership (although, incidentally, the rite does include the historic laying on of hands of the newly baptized). Once again *it is the liturgical expression that makes clear what we believe*. It says so in unequivocal terms.

"Christian Baptism and Church Membership: An Essay on the Ministry of the People of God and an Example of a Service of Affirmation and of Reaffirmation of Faith" (Parts 3 & 4) (1994) (see p.104 below)

There is one final thing, however, at least so far as our picture of a uniting church becomes clearer. If it is by baptism that someone is admitted into the church, what about that other rite of passage often called "confirmation", or "adult membership", or — even less satisfactorily — "full membership" (as if to imply that some are only half-members or perhaps quarter-members)?

This is where our latest report and liturgical rite comes in. Just published as parts 3 and 4 of our report on "Christian Baptism and Church Membership" this delivers on the promise undertaken in its earlier parts for "A Service of Affirmation (or Reaffirmation) of Faith". This now is all about *applying in practice* the vows undertaken in baptism to be a good soldier of Jesus Christ and his faithful disciple.

It provides for personal affirmation of faith — or reaffirmation, for there is surely no limit to the times that are appropriate for declaring our allegiance to Christ and making specific promises for service. The intention of this rite is to provide a framework for considerably varied and flexible content, the archetype, if you like, of any one of a number of commitment occasions — ordination, induction, appointment to church office — even the opportunity for renewal of someone returning to the fold after "lapsed" membership. Once again it is experimental and even now just before the churches for use and comment. But, like the baptismal rite this rite of affirmation *is being used*. We are, at the very least, trying to say what we mean and mean what we say.

Only time will tell how successful we are with these tools of unity, for that is what they are. If the covenanting churches continue to choose their own traditional rites they will by that token be expressing what they believe. But it is then arguable that this is not altogether consistent with what each of our churches said we meant when we undertook to "covenant together" "to work and pray...[to] be brought into one visible church". Remember that warning given at the outset of the ministry report that

> the churches must resist the temptation to see the uniting church of the future as their own denomination writ large and to ask other churches to change in order to fit in with their present self-understanding and pattern. Instead each must ask of itself: How can we be renewed and changed in order to receive God's gift of unity?

I must return at last to the realism of the bishop's remark to which I referred earlier. What is here is "a challenge to the churches", something of a rainbow which contains all that is good in the varied colours of many traditions. To some it will seem "streets ahead" of where they are, and it is very hard work actually selling these practical proposals. Yet the churches in Wales know all too well to their cost that "the disease of indolence and indifference" *is* mortal. Many dark clouds hang over them and they long for better days. Let the picture be bright and full of imagination for it is God's promise — ENFYS, the rainbow of the covenant. Let us see what we discover of ourselves and others, and of the promise of God, when we actually "say what we mean and mean what we say".

* * *

TEXTS

THE COVENANT

This is the text of the Covenant signed in 1975 by the Church in Wales, the Presbyterian Church of Wales, the Methodist Church, the United Reformed Church and a number of Baptist Churches.

CONFESSING OUR FAITH IN JESUS CHRIST AS LORD AND SAVIOUR, and renewing our will to serve his mission in the world, our several churches have been brought into a new relationship with one another. Together we give thanks for all we have in common. Together we repent the sin of perpetuating our division. Together we make known our understanding of the obedience to which we are called:

1. a) We recognize in one another the same faith in the gospel of Jesus Christ found in holy scripture, which the creeds of the ancient church and other historic confessions are intended to safeguard. We recognize in one another the same desire to hold this faith in its fullness.
   b) We intend so to act, speak and serve together in obedience to the gospel that we may learn more of its fullness and make it known to others in contemporary terms and by credible witness.
2. a) We recognize in one another the same awareness of God's calling to serve his gracious purpose for all mankind, with particular responsibility for this land and people.
   b) We intend to work together for justice and peace at home and abroad, and for the spiritual and material well-being and personal freedom of all people.
3. a) We recognize one another as within the one church of Jesus Christ, pledged to serve his kingdom, and sharing in the unity of the Spirit.
   b) We intend by the help of the same Spirit to overcome the divisions which impair our witness, impede God's mission, and obscure the gospel of man's salvation, and to manifest that unity which is in accordance with Christ's will.
4. a) We recognize the members of all our churches as members of Christ in virtue of their common baptism and common calling to participate in the ministry of the whole church.
   b) We intend to seek that form of common life which will enable each member to use the gifts bestowed on him in the service of Christ's kingdom.
5. a) We recognize the ordained ministries of all our churches as true ministries of the word and sacraments, through which God's love is proclaimed, his grace mediated, and his fatherly care exercised.
   b) We intend to seek an agreed pattern of ordained ministry which will serve the gospel in unity, manifest its continuity throughout the ages, and be accepted as far as may be by the church throughout the world.
6. a) We recognize in one another patterns of worship and sacramental life, marks of holiness and zeal, which are manifestly gifts of Christ.
   b) We intend to listen to one another and to study together the witness and practice of our various traditions, in order that the riches entrusted to us in separation may be preserved for the united church which we seek.
7. a) We recognize in one another the same concern for the good government of the church for the fulfilment of its mission.
   b) We intend to seek a mode of church government which will preserve the positive values for which each has stood, so that the common mind of the church may be formed and carried into action through constitutional organs of corporate decision at every level of responsibility.

We do not yet know the form union will take. We approach our task with openness to the Spirit. We believe that God will guide his church into ways of truth and peace, correcting, strengthening, and renewing it in accordance with the mind of Christ. We therefore urge all our members to accept one another in the Holy Spirit as Jesus Christ accepts us, and to avail themselves of every opportunity to grow together through common prayer and worship in mutual understanding and love so that in every place they may be renewed together for mission.

Accordingly we enter now into this solemn covenant before God and with one another, to work and pray in common obedience to our Lord Jesus Christ, in order that by the Holy Spirit we may be brought into one visible church to serve together in mission to the glory of God the Father.

The Methodist Church
The Church in Wales
The United Reformed Church
The Presbyterian Church of Wales
The Covenanted Baptist Churches

PRINCIPLES OF VISIBLE UNITY IN WALES (1980)

This report set out for discussion the theological issues covered by the seven dual clauses of the 1974 covenant.

In the introduction it was emphasized that "it is intended as a discussion, consultative document only; it is not a scheme of union. Therefore, we invite the churches to study the document at national, regional and local levels and to bring to the commission as full a response as is possible to the details of the principles outlined... It is hoped that this document will assist the churches to discover what they hold in common so that they may through their life and work proclaim Christ to the glory of God, Father, Son and Holy Spirit."

Each section began by quoting the relevant clauses and then expanding them in a theological text. In each case it concluded with a summary expressing the likely position of the uniting church of the future — although clearly open for debate by the participating churches before the event.

These summary statements were as follows:

1. Faith. The Uniting Church of Wales confesses the faith which the church universal has ever held in one God, Father, Son and Holy Spirit. It acknowledges the word of God in the Old and New Testaments, discerned through the continuing guidance of the Holy Spirit, as the supreme authority for belief and obedience. It acknowledges that salvation is God's gift through Jesus Christ, received by grace through faith. It thus understands itself as inheritor of the fullness of the tradition of the church, Catholic, Reformed and Evangelical.

2. Mission. The Uniting Church of Wales accepts its responsibility to further God's mission in the world, both by corporate action and by the individual initiative of its members. It sees its visible unity as a gift from God to be used to his glory in making known to all peoples, by word and action.

3. The nature of the church. The Uniting Church of Wales, believing itself to be within the one, holy, catholic and apostolic church of Jesus Christ, accepts its responsibility to maintain the fullness of the universal church. It also gives expression to the legitimate desire for local freedom and diversity in the enrichment of church life.

4. Membership. At the inauguration of union every member of each of the churches will be a member of the Uniting Church. Membership of the Uniting Church of Wales is open to all who are baptized into the name of the Holy Trinity, who confess Jesus Christ as Lord and Saviour, and who accept the obligation to serve God faithfully in the life of the church and in the world.

5. Ministry. The Uniting Church of Wales receives with thanksgiving the ordained ministries of all the covenanted churches, uniting them into a single pattern of ministry for the service of the gospel in this land. Witnessing to its continuity with the universal church throughout the ages, it retains the threefold ministry of bishops, presbyters and deacons. It believes that this pattern of ministry, renewed for mission, is capable of serving the wider unity of the church, both in Wales and throughout the world.

6. Worship. The Uniting Church of Wales intends to retain the widest possible diversity in patterns of worship that is consistent with unity in the service of the gospel. It encourages its congregations to draw upon all the riches entrusted to the churches in their separation. It also encourages its congregations so to act that linguistic differences do not become a cause of disunity.

7. Church government. The Uniting Church of Wales recognizes that government is the function of the whole people of God, guided by the Spirit and acting corporately in true partnership. Within this partnership each order and level has its own particular insights and responsibilities. The constitution will secure the rights of individuals and congregations within an ordered structure in such a way that each may make its proper contribution to the life of the whole, in order that the mission of God to the people of Wales may be served effectively.

THE HOLY COMMUNION (1981)

Foreword

The order for the holy communion now presented is intended to be used on the occasion of joint communion services of the Covenanted Churches in Wales. If its use is thus limited, it nevertheless represents a major step towards union on the part of the churches involved.

No one should minimize the difficulties that have been faced in producing this order. For all of us the rite involves changes in, or omission from, our traditional forms and orders: the reasons for each change and every omission may be regarded with some suspicion. During our work we have sometimes been able to realize that doctrinal difference could be used in a complementary way, to enrich rather than to separate. Even where this was not possible we have endeavoured to include rather than to exclude, recognizing nevertheless that the doctrinal tensions will still exist.

Whilst the "shape" of the rite follows the pattern most widely found in our separate modern traditions, it is our assertion that the key to our work is to be found in the great thanksgiving over the bread and the wine and that this prayer stands in the very long tradition of such prayers and theologically brings us together.

(The foreword went on to refer to sources, and urged careful preparation on each occasion. The notes of direction then set out the best way to ensure that the service flow smoothly, with suggestions over such things as posture, methods of communicating, etc. It also stated:) "4. Minister: The service should be presided over by an ordained minister of one of the covenanted churches. At the point of thanksgiving and communion such presidency should be shared by ordained ministers representing the several denominations present."

THE HOLY COMMUNION: SUPPLEMENT (1993)

This booklet provides alternative forms for the gloria (including music), the intercessions, the peace (including music), and gives appropriate (seasonal) prefaces for the thanksgiving.

The introduction stresses: "It is hoped that the existence of this supplement will also give encouragement to those who may wish to find other appropriate variants, to do so, without detracting from the fundamental shape and authority of the original text."

THE HOLY COMMUNION (1981)
COVENANTED CHURCHES OF WALES

Notes of direction, collects and other additional material are published separately under the title "Prayers and Directions".

THE PREPARATION

Stand *A hymn may be sung*

Minister: O come, let us worship and bow down,
let us kneel before the Lord, our Maker.

**All: For he is our God and we are the people of his pasture
and the sheep of his hand.**

Kneel/sit Let us pray

Almighty God, to whom all hearts are open, all desires known and from whom no secrets are hidden; cleanse the thoughts of our hearts by the inspiration of your Holy Spirit, that we may perfectly love you, and worthily magnify your holy Name; through Christ our Lord. Amen.

Let us confess our sins to Almighty God:

Merciful God, we confess that we have sinned against you in thought, word and deed; we have not loved you with all our heart; we have not loved our neighbour as ourselves. We are sorry for all our sins and truly repent. Father, forgive us and by the power of your Spirit help us to renounce sin, enable us to forgive others, keep us in your ways of truth and love, that we may grow up into Christ and serve you in newness of live; through Jesus Christ, our Lord. Amen.

Receive this assurance:
"There is therefore now no condemnation for those who are in Christ Jesus." Our sins are forgiven in Christ.

Amen. Thanks be to God.

Stand *The gloria may be said or sung*

Glory to God in the highest, and peace to his people on earth. Lord God, heavenly King, Almighty God and Father, we worship you, we give you thanks, we praise you for your glory. Lord Jesus Christ, only Son of the Father, Lord God, Lamb of God, you take away the sins of the world: have mercy on us; you are seated at the right hand of the Father: receive our prayer. For you alone are the Holy One, you alone are the Lord, you alone are the Most High, Jesus Christ, with the Holy Spirit, in the glory of God the Father. Amen.

Or a hymn may be sung

THE MINISTRY OF THE WORD

Sit *A collect or prayer may be said*
The Old Testament lesson
The epistle

Stand The gospel

We praise you, God,
We acknowledge you to be the Lord.

Sit *The Nicene Creed*

We believe in one God, the Father, the Almighty, maker of heaven and earth, of all that is, seen and unseen. We believe in one Lord, Jesus Christ, the only Son of God, eternally begotten of the Father, God from God, Light from Light, true God from true God, begotten, not made, of one Being with the Father. Through him all things were made. For us and for our salvation he came down from heaven; by the power of the Holy Spirit he became incarnate from the Virgin Mary and was made man. For our sake he was crucified under Pontius Pilate, he suffered death and was buried. On the third day he rose again in accordance with the scriptures; he ascended into heaven and is seated at the right hand of the Father. He will come again in glory to judge the living and the dead: and his kingdom will have no end.

We believe in the Holy Spirit, the Lord, the Giver of Life, who proceeds from the Father and the Son. With the Father and Son he is worshipped and glorified. He has spoken through the prophets.

We believe in one holy catholic and apostolic church. We acknowledge one baptism for the forgiveness of sins. We look for the resurrection of the dead, and the life of the world to come. Amen.

Kneel/sit Let us pray
For the peace that is from above, and for the salvation
of all, let us pray to the Lord:
Lord, hear our prayer.

For the peace of the whole world, for the welfare of God's holy church, and for the unity of all, let us pray to the Lord:
Lord, hear our prayer.

For the ministers of all the churches (especially...), that with a good heart and a pure conscience they may accomplish their ministry, let us pray to the Lord:
Lord, hear our prayer.

For the rulers of our country and all in authority (especially...), let us pray to the Lord:
Lord, hear our prayer.

For the sick, the suffering, the lonely, the sorrowful, and the dying (especially...), let us pray to the Lord:
Lord, hear our prayer.

For the poor, the hungry, the homeless and those who suffer persecution (especially...), let us pray to the Lord:
Lord, hear our prayer.

For ourselves and all who confess the name of Christ (especially...), that we may proclaim the triumphs of him who called us out of darkness into his marvellous light, let us pray to the Lord:
Lord, hear our prayer.

That, with all his servants who have served him here and are now at rest (especially...), we may enter into the fullness of his unending joy, let us pray to the Lord:
Lord, hear our prayer. Amen.

(or the minister offers intercession in his or her own words for the church and the world)

THE MINISTRY OF THE SACRAMENT

Stand *The minister may say:*

We are the body of Christ.
In the one Spirit we were all baptized into one body.
Let us then pursue all that makes for
peace and builds up our common life.

The minister shares the peace with the congregation, saying:

The peace of the Lord be always with you.
And also with you.

The collection is brought forward
The presiding minister takes bread and wine
The words of institution may be read

Stand The Lord is here
His Spirit is with us

Life up your hearts
We lift them to the Lord

Let us give thanks to the Lord our God
It is right to give him thanks and praise

Therefore, with all your creation in heaven and on earth we proclaim your great and glorious name, for ever praising you, and saying
Holy, holy, holy Lord,
God of power and might,
heaven and earth are full of your glory;
Hosanna in the highest.

We praise you, Almighty Father, for creating all things and for making us in your own image. We thank you that while we were yet sinners you gave your only Son, Jesus Christ, to live as one of us, to suffer death on the cross and to rise again for our salvation. On the night he was betrayed he took bread and, after giving thanks to you, he broke it and gave it to his disciples saying, "Take, eat; this is my body which is for you; do this in remembrance of me." In the same way, he took the cup after supper, saying, "Drink from this, all of you; this cup is the new covenant in my blood. Whenever you drink it, do this in remembrance of me."
Christ has died;
Christ is risen;
Christ will come again.

Therefore, heavenly Father, as we now proclaim his death, resurrection and ascension we offer to you these your gifts of bread and wine and ask you to accept our sacrifice of praise and thanksgiving. We pray that your Holy Spirit may come upon us and upon these gifts that we, receiving them, may share the body and blood of our Lord and be united in peace and love with all your faithful people, through the same Jesus Christ, by whom, in whom and with whom in the unity of the Holy Spirit, all honour and glory are yours, Almighty Father, now and for ever. Amen.

Kneel/sit **Our Father in heaven, hallowed be your Name, your kingdom come, your will be done, on earth as in heaven. Give us today our daily bread; Forgive us our sins as we forgive those who sin against us. Lead us not into temptation but deliver us from evil. For the kingdom, the power, and the glory are yours now and for ever. Amen.**

The minister breaks the bread and says

The bread which we break is it not a communion in the body of Christ?
Because there is one bread, we who are many are one body, for we all partake of the one bread.

The minister lifts the cup and says

The cup of blessing which we bless, is it not a communion in the blood of Christ?

The minister and other communicants share and receive the sacramental bread and wine, with the words,

The body of Christ, the Bread of Life,
The blood of Christ, the True Vine.

Each communicant responds: Amen.

Any consecrated bread and wine which is not required for purposes of communion is consumed at the end of the administration, or after the service.

Either or both of the following prayers are said

The minister says:

Father of all, we give you thanks and praise, that when we were still far off you met us in your Son and brought us home. Dying and living, he declared your love, gave us grace and opened the gate of glory. May we who share Christ's body live his risen life; we who drink his cup bring life to others; we whom the Spirit lights give light to others. Keep us in this hope that we have grasped; so we and all your children shall be free and the whole earth live to praise your name; through Christ our Lord. Amen.

Almighty God, we thank you for feeding us with the body and blood of your Son, Jesus Christ. Through him we offer you our souls and bodies to be a living sacrifice. Send us out in the power of your Spirit to live and work to your praise and glory. Amen.

Stand *A hymn is sung*

The minister says:

The blessing of God Almighty, the Father, the Son and the Holy Spirit, be among you, and remain with you always.

or

The grace of our Lord Jesus Christ and the love of God and the fellowship of the Holy Spirit be with us all. Amen.

Go in peace and serve the Lord.
In the name of Christ. Amen.

MINISTRY IN A UNITING CHURCH FROM RECOGNITION TO RECONCILIATION (1986)

This report was based on clause 5 of the covenant, which states:

> We recognize the ordained ministries of all our churches as true ministries of the word and sacraments, through which God's love is proclaimed, his grace mediated and his fatherly care exercised.
>
> We intend to seek an agreed pattern of ordained ministry which will serve the gospel in unity, manifest its continuity throughout the ages, and be accepted as far as may be by the church throughout the world.

In *Part One: The Pattern of Ministry* it considered the ministry of the whole people of God and went on to deal with practical matters of geography and the exercise of a variety of ministries, including the historic threefold order of ordained ministries.

In *Part Two: Inaugurating a New Pattern of Ministries* it reflected on various schemes of union and then went on to suggest a way forward towards the mutual reconciliation of ministries and the inauguration of a uniting church.

On page 33 para. 78 the report stated: "It remains for us to give some outline to the means by which such a scheme might be inaugurated. The commission is at present working on a fuller draft of *an act of inauguration* and hopes to make this available to the churches by the end of 1986."

Finally the report posed *four questions* to which it invited the churches to respond concerning these proposals. But in the introduction it had warned:

"In this discussion process the churches must resist the temptation to see the uniting church of the future as their own denomination writ large and to ask other churches to change in order to fit in with their present self-understanding and pattern. Instead each must ask of itself: How can we be renewed and changed in order to receive God's gift of unity?"

* * *

The responses to this report were extremely complex, as had been predicted. No churches answered unequivocally "yes", but neither did any church turn the proposals down with a categorical "no". Instead, more questions were raised and the Commission is at present working on the promise that this presents — particularly at present with the idea of *an ecumenical (missionary) episcopate*.

THE INAUGURATION OF A UNITING CHURCH IN WALES DRAFT SERVICES (1987)

The Introduction began:

"1. It has long been recognized that the clearest expression of what Christians believe is to be found in the way they worship. In *Ministry in a Uniting Church (MIUC) (para. 78, page 33)*, the commission undertook to prepare a draft act of inauguration for a Uniting Church in Wales, based on the service used at the inauguration of the Church of North India. It was our hope that in providing such a draft, which at this stage might seem simply an academic exercise (because it will, after all, be some years before the churches are in a position to engage in such an act) we will actually have gone some way in clarifying the theology of ministry which underpins the proposals contained in MIUC. However, in preparing this draft it has become apparent that this clarification can only be achieved when the laying on of hands which takes place as part of the act of inauguration can be compared with the laying on of hands when it is used in a service of ordination."

This book then set out:

An Act of Inauguration, starting with an act of unification of the churches. Consequent upon that there takes place an act in which the ministries of the participating churches are reconciled and unified.

An Order for the Ordination of Deacons, Presbyters and Bishops. This is an order which might be used as part of the inauguration of a uniting church and thereafter.

A Service of Thanksgiving to be used thereafter in each diocese of the Uniting Church — an integral part of inauguration.

The Act of Inauguration includes the following:

- An Act of Unification of Churches:
  - Introductory Statement
  - Prayer of Confession
  - Presentation of the Participating Churches' Resolutions
  - Prayer of Inauguration
  - Declaration of Inauguration
- Ministry of the Word, including readings, sermon, creed
- The Representative Act of Reconciliation and Unification of Ministries:
  - Preface
  - Presentation of Representative Ministers
  - Declaration by Representative Ministers
  - Prayer by the Representative Leaders

"22. The Reconciliation of Ministries

The five representative leaders stand in line (in the order Baptist, Church in Wales, Methodist, Presbyterian and United Reformed) facing the Lord's table. Beginning with the Baptist representative, each of the five leaders in turn shall lay hands upon the head of each of the other four, saying the following words, and taking his/her place at the other end of the line thereafter.

> 'May God continue his blessing already given in your ordination; may he use our action here for the reconciliation of all our ministries within the Uniting Church in Wales.'

"23. The Reconciliation of Representative Ministers

Those who have been presented as representative ministers of the participating churches shall then come forward as representatives of the new dioceses of the Uniting Church, diocese by diocese in alphabetical order. These will, from each diocese, include the bishop-designate as well as those who will be presbyters and deacons in the Uniting Church.

The five representative leaders shall lay hands in turn upon the head of each, with the following words:

(As above)"

Ascription of Praise
Ministry of the Sacrament

(At the end of the proposals for this service and before that for the future ordination of deacons, presbyters and bishops, there was added an appendix giving details of the particular thinking that lay behind the method of reconciliation used above.)

CHRISTIAN BAPTISM AND CHURCH MEMBERSHIP: A RITE OF BAPTISM FOR THE COVENANTED CHURCHES AND AN ESSAY ON BAPTISM AND MEMBERSHIP (1990)[1]

This rite and essay were based on clause 4 of the covenant, which states:

> We recognize the members of all our churches as members of Christ in virtue of their common baptism and common calling to participate in the ministry of the whole church.
>
> We intend to seek that form of common life which will enable each member to use the gifts bestowed on him/her in the service of Christ's kingdom.

The Introduction makes clear that this rite and essay bring together two methods of approach — the *practical one* of the style of the holy communion, *to be used now wherever possible*, and the *theoretical one* of studying a theological argument in the style of ministry in a uniting church.

Like that report, it concluded with four questions put to the churches for considered response, based on *their use and study of this material.*

"4. It is hoped that as a minimum it will be authorized as an occasional alternative form to present denominational rites; particularly, for example, where a candidate for believer's baptism is particularly responsive to the aims of the covenant, or where the parents of a child presented for baptism do not themselves come from a common denominational background. We believe that there is nothing here that conflicts with the doctrinal basis of any of the forms currently used within our churches, only in the way that doctrine is expressed. And so where this rite differs in such expression it invites reflection within the parameters of the doctrine of 'one baptism'.

"5. It is further hoped that this rite may gradually become an alternative and a replacement to denominational practices and in this way will demonstrate the unity we have discovered in our understanding of baptism. If such services are planned and celebrated jointly in a given locality — whether very occasionally or as a regular practice — this rite of Christian baptism, like the rite of the holy communion of the Covenanted Churches in Wales, can be both the means of growing together and an expression of our growth towards a uniting church."

In "Part One: The Baptismal Liturgy — an Experimental Rite", an order of service was given set in the context of "The Holy Communion (1981) Rite", together with notes on its use — pointing out that it was a *common order* for both believers' baptism (which should be taken as the norm) and infant baptism.

The liturgy of baptism comes at the point of the confession of faith, following the word proclaimed. Following the Nicene Creed or another recognized credal statement the scriptural warrant is read, concluding with the words:

> Christian baptism thus derives from the baptism of Jesus which foreshadowed the cross. What took place in the river Jordan is inseparable from the death and resurrection of Jesus, and the invitation to baptism and discipleship is nothing less than a call to die with Christ and to rise again with him. It is a sign of the forgiveness of our sins and the seal of

> our new relationship with God, accomplished through the cross and resurrection. By this sacrament we are made one in the body of Christ, his church, and receive the gift of the Holy Spirit, to enable us to live as the people of God and to serve his purpose in the world.

In the case of infant baptism the statement continues:

> Children who are too young to profess for themselves the Christian faith are baptized in the context of their upbringing as Christians within the family of the church and in expectation that in due course they will make their own confession of faith. As they grow up, they need the help and encouragement of that family, so that they learn to be faithful in Christian worship, to live by trust in God and, by the leading of the Holy Spirit, to come to believe and confess that Jesus is Lord and to commit their lives to his service. It is of the utmost importance, therefore, that in acting in respect of the children and in undertaking to provide for his/her spiritual nurture, all those who have responsibility for him/her present themselves solemnly before God, whose grace alone is sufficient for such a charge.

(Apart from this addition the content of the service is common to both infants' and believers' baptism, but it does include material that is "new" for all at one point or another.)

"Part Two: Baptism and Membership — An Explanatory Essay" on belonging to the church and being incorporated into the body of Christ argues that baptism denotes (full) membership and nothing needs to be added, as should be seen from the liturgical text. However, the essay points the way to further consideration of the *implications of membership (discipleship)* and promises that this will be further developed in a subsequent report.

CHRISTIAN BAPTISM AND CHURCH MEMBERSHIP: AN ESSAY ON THE MINISTRY OF THE PEOPLE OF GOD AND AN EXAMPLE OF A SERVICE OF AFFIRMATION AND OF REAFFIRMATION OF FAITH (1994)[2]

This essay and rite, together with an appendix on confirmation, children and communion, and one on a programme of pre-commitment training, is also based on clause 4 of the covenant considered in parts one and two, and provides parts three and four of the study on baptism and membership.

Part Three: The Ministry of the People of God — a further essay on church membership takes further the earlier essay in considering the implications of membership — the practical responsibilities involved. This is all the more important since it was pointed out that the report "Ministry in a Uniting Church" gave promise of the consideration of the ministry of the whole people of God and then developed only that of the ordained ministry.

This sequel recalls the quotation from the WCC second assembly at Evanston in 1954 on the vital role of the members of the body of Christ in ministering to the world:

> The laity are not mere fragments of the church who are scattered about in the world and who come together again for worship, instruction and specifically Christian fellowship on Sundays. They are Christ's representatives, no matter where they are. It is the laity who draw together work and worship: it is they who bridge the gulf between the church and the world, and it is they who manifest in word and action the Lordship of Christ over that world which claims so much of their time and energy and labour. This, and not some new order or organization, is the ministry of the laity.

In developing this, the essay argues that it should be possible and it is desirable to express *the ministry of the people of God liturgically*, and that such a service of commitment — over and above the Christian initiation in baptism — should include:

- a statement of personal belief, and recognition of the call of Christ to follow him wherever he commands;
- a rehearsal of the nature of the body of Christ and the various gifts of the Holy Spirit;
- an undertaking of promises, borne up with the supporting faith of the church;
- the laying on of hands with a prayer for constant renewal and the strength of the Holy Spirit to live as part of Christ's present and coming kingdom;
- the provision of a variety of means of expressing a reaffirmation of faith for both individuals and entire congregations.

Part Four: An Example of a Service of Affirmation and of Reaffirmation of Faith adds one more to the liturgies so far produced within the covenant to express our intention to grow together in commitment to the mission of God.

Like that of baptism, it is set in the context of the holy communion, with the *Liturgy of Commitment* coming at the point of expressing the faith credally.

In alternative forms — and in this service it is particularly emphasized that there can be considerable variety within the framework to give particular contemporary expression — the vows of baptism are recalled, followed by an act of contrition and (re)affirmation of faith in Christ and commitment to (specific acts of) discipleship.

The key words at the laying on of hands are:

> Renew and strengthen, O Lord, your servant N... with your Holy Spirit and direct him/her in the service of your kingdom. Amen.

It is arguable whether this service is to be seen as a replacement for confirmation or whether it has already been argued that there is no need for confirmation in any case. The report therefore adds an *Appendix on Confirmation and Children and Communion*, along the same lines that baptism denotes (full) membership, whilst not itself trying to go beyond the debates which are taking place in the churches on these subjects already. What is proposed here is a logical progression of pursuing the clauses of the covenant to which all the churches are already committed.

Like the previous reports, this too poses questions to be considered in the light of experience. *It does not set out a definitive position.* Rather, it offers material and especially *liturgical rites* — which may help the churches in their search for unity.

NOTES

[1] Also available is the text "Baptism", which is "the rite on its own without the detailed notes of explanation but in the same format as the holy communion service in which it is set and intended for congregational use".

[2] Also available is a "Service of Affirmation and of Reaffirmation of Faith". This is "the rite on its own without the detailed notes of explanation set in a form intended for congregational use".

III

The Worship Life of the Consultation

"Blessed Is the One Who Will Eat at the Feast in the Kingdom of God"

Homily at the Opening Worship

ZACHARIAS MAR THEOPHILUS

Text: Luke 14:15-24 (the parable of the great banquet)

St Luke's gospel is unique in its universalism and inclusivism. This parable is a classic example of the same qualities. Jesus is in a Pharisee's house sharing in a banquet, an event which has an eschatological significance for it alludes to the future banquet with the Messiah. The context is the comment by one of the participants: "Blessed is the one who will eat at the feast in the kingdom of God." Jesus takes this opportunity to define, through a beautiful parable, who would be in his kingdom and what would be the criteria for entry into the kingdom.

In the parable, a Master is inviting his chosen people to eat with him and to meet with one another. Eating and meeting are two aspects of friendship and fellowship. There is a relationship and intimacy for which dear ones are called. But all the invited guests rejected the invitation. In other words, they kept away or opted out from the intimacy with the Master and the fellowship with the other persons.

They could find sound and reasonable excuses for their aloofness. The first one seeks to be excused on the ground that he has "just bought a field and must go and see it". In one way that is very reasonable. Land is the means of production. He must possess it. That is his asset, the basis of his economic prosperity. Very often material prosperity keeps many away from the joy of the Master. The modern consumerist society forces us to opt out from the communion with God and with his people.

The second invited guest says that he has "just bought five yokes of oxen and he is on his way to try them out". In those days in the East, the number of oxen was the measure of social position, a symbol of power and popularity. Even today, to acquire power and to keep up one's position is a strong urge among many. Our struggles and constant wars mar the face of earth. In this competitive society, where each one wants to be his own master, the call of the Master to a common banquet is rejected.

The third invitee keeps away from the banquet on the grounds that he "just got married and so he cannot come". To be with the newly-wed wife is only natural. Family bonds are very important. Moments of personal pleasure could not be postponed or delayed. People today think they should enjoy — here and now — any experience which they will find satisfying. There also the Master's call is side-tracked. Personal pleasure finds priority over corporate enjoyment.

All three opted out of the joy of the Master. Each one had his own private agenda. Their priorities were different. They could find both lame excuses and good reasons.

The immediate, private and personal took priority over the lasting, corporate and divine. Even now the questions of private agenda and personal priorities prompt many to opt out from the great banquet, where all come together in gratitude and gladness around the table with the Master.

The Master is pained, grieved and angered at the rejection, as any one who had been rejected would be. But he widens his invitation to the poor, crippled, blind and lame who stray in the streets and alleys. Now the door is open to the weak, ignored, faceless and marginalized people, and all find an entry. The servant reports that there is still more space! Therefore all who were roaming in the roads and lanes were invited, so that the banquet room is full. The people at the periphery are brought into the mainstream. The marginalized are centralized. The kingdom's door is open to the chosen and the marginalized. The banquet is open to all; you can either opt out or come in.

Jesus makes very clear the answer to the question, who would be in the kingdom. The first would be the last, and would become the lost; the last would be the first, as those who had been lost were found. The values of the kingdom, and the criteria for entering it, are distinct and different from those of the world. In the kingdom of God there is always room for everyone. The chosen and the invited may opt out of the banquet, while the ignored and uninvited may find a prime place in it.

The eucharist is indeed a communion with God and a koinonia with God's people. When the Master calls, will we opt out from the fellowship with him and with God's people? Let us pray for the eucharistic moment when none will opt out or will be kept out from the great joy around the table of the Master. May God bless us that we may rejoice in this world where all God's people will be together at the broken bread and the poured wine in love, joy and peace — a real foretaste of the Heavenly Banquet.

"That They May All Be One... That the World May Believe"

Homily at the Eucharist

GORDON LATHROP

Jeremiah 33:6-9a, John 17:1,11b-27

Dear sisters in Christ: I am afraid that this Faith and Order consultation has been something of a disorder among you. It is not only that we have not known quite how to keep the silence of the *caesura* while trying to sing the psalms with you in Compline each night. It is much more that we have filled the peace of your hallways and grounds — even of your offices until late at night! — with the vigorous and sometimes confused sounds of our work. Now however, by your kindness and hospitality, the disorder is set aside. We are all gathered in peaceful array around this holy book and this holy table.

But, dear sisters and brothers in Christ, we all come here from a much larger disorder than the one we have occasioned here. We come from disunited churches, from a radically disordered, even dismembered world. These disorders are not so easily set aside even by gracious hospitality.

Then let this day — this Thursday, day of the supper, day of the new commandment of love, day of weekly prayer for Christian unity in this community — let this day indeed be as an island of hope amid such disorder, a prayer for unity, a candle burning before God in beseeching. Or, rather, let the prayer which fills this day be Christ's own prayer "that they may all be one... that the world may believe". Let that prayer become the prayer of our hearts. And let those words bring to expression the agonies of the world, admitting into our own hearts and mouths the cries for unity and reconciliation and justice which arise from human life everywhere. Let our prayer be for that unity of the church which should be a foreshadowing of the healing of the wounds of the world itself.

But hear this: such prayer has an answer. The name of the unity of the church is in Jesus Christ. He who prays is also he who washes feet and, serving, makes those whom he serves to be part of himself. He who prays is also he who is lifted up and, on the cross, draws all to himself. In the cross, Christ has taken far more disorder into himself — far more agony than we can imagine or admit into our beseeching prayer. All disorder, all agony, all longing for unity had been taken into the cross — and, in the resurrection, healed! Henceforth, there is no falling which is not falling into him, no cry for unity and peace where he is not already present.

And he is raised up. Jesus Christ, the risen one, is in you. And the Father is in him. And all are bound together in the love of the Spirit, as the beginning of the healing of harms, the foreshadowing of unity for all the world. Such a unity is now given, here, already.

How?

By this word in your ears, sinking into your hearts. In this word, Christ comes to you now, draws you to his cross, serves you in footwashing love, shares your own agonies and death, and so makes you part of him and thus part of each other, one with all those who hear this faith-creating word.

But also, this unity is given now by the bodily presence of your sisters and brothers around you, before you. These concrete persons — the ones you now see — are the very dwelling place of Christ's word, and thus they are the dwelling place of the Holy Trinity, the centre and model of all unity. Behold them! You see the very body of Christ, against all our disunities. In this little, fragile company, there is, by God's mercy, already now, the very city of joy, washed by God and set forth for the world.

And there is even more: if you can, this unity is given now in the holy bread and cup given into your hands and mouth and life. He who feeds us with himself is himself our unity and the end of our divisions. Or — do you see?! — even if the state of our disunity means that you cannot now come to this supper, our pain and our divisions are also now *in him*! Underneath our division, he is our unity. For now, as we pray in him, some of us eat and drink for you. While you refrain — holding our circle open, telling the truth about our disunity — you refrain *for us*. But Christ — Christ who gathers all disorder and agony to himself, Christ of the word, Christ of the bodily presence of other believers, Christ of the bread and cup, the one Christ — is himself our unity.

So are we being made into God's city of joy for the world.

Dear sisters and brothers: today, yourselves be the prayer for unity. But be also, already, the city of joy, a word for the world, that they may believe.

Amen.

The Worship Life of the Consultation: An Example of Inculturation

At this consultation on the theme "Towards Koinonia in Worship" we not only discussed questions of worship, but also tried to "live" what we discussed. Thus a lively worship life formed the framework within which we spent our six days together. This common experience in worship drew us into communion in God and with one another, and this in turn undergirded — and enriched — our reflections.

- The beginning of the consultation was marked by an opening eucharistic service. Held in the chapel of the guest house, this was celebrated according to a shortened form of the "Lima liturgy".
- Early each morning the participants were free to join the sisters of the Community of All Hallows at eucharist in the convent chapel. One morning each week this service focuses upon Christian unity. We joined the sisters on this occasion, with members of the consultation participating in the service.
- At noon, in the chapel of the guest house, the consultation held its common mid-day prayer.
- Each evening we joined the sisters in the convent chapel for their service of compline.
- The closing service was according to the order of the breaking of the bread from the Orthodox tradition. This was held in the chapel of the guest house.
- We also worshipped briefly in the church and cell of Julian of Norwich, and participated in sung Anglican evensong at Norwich cathedral. Though not a part of the regular worship life of our consultation, these experiences greatly enriched our life and work.

The worship leaders — as well as the congregation as a whole — came from different traditions, cultures and contexts, with each bringing their background and experiences into the context of this consultation. Thus our common life of praise and prayer became itself a lively example of the inculturation of worship. To illustrate this we include here the texts of the services prepared directly for the consultation, together with a brief explanation of their structure and content.

The Opening Worship
Sunday, 21 August 1994

At the opening worship the presiding officer was Bishop Zacharias Mar Theophilus of the Mar Thoma Church, India, with many other participants also involved in leadership.

The service was a celebration of the Lima liturgy in a shortened and simplified form. The order of service had been shortened in such a way that the structure and main elements remained. In the entrance the kyrie litany was removed, and the kyrie was put after the confession to represent the congregation's confirmation of the words of confession spoken by the minister. The gloria after the absolution, then, is understood as a thanksgiving or praise to the Lord for the remission of sins.

There were only two biblical readings and, in this case, no creed. Epiclesis I and II were combined and placed after the anamnesis in order to avoid a "magical" or merely functional understanding of epiclesis I. The anamnesis was shortened, and passages which could be understood as repetitions were taken out. The same principle was used in shortening the commemorations. The bread was broken during the words of institution, and therefore the reference to 1 Corinthians 10:16-17 before communion was omitted.

There are, of course, other possibilities for shortening and simplifying the Lima liturgy, as was already forseen when the text was originally published[1] (see also the account of reflections on the Lima liturgy in appendix 1 to the report of the consultation, p.22 in this volume).

Our principle in simplifying the service was to keep its fundamental structure, namely the balance between liturgy of the word and liturgy of the eucharist, each mutually referring to the other: the word of God leads us to the celebration of the eucharist, and the eucharist cannot be celebrated without the word of God. The two are linked by the intercessions, that part of the liturgy where the world is brought into the worship service and before God. In some cases the texts were shortened; only in one case an addition was made (in the commemorations, a reference to the "whole people" was added as, although the logic of the prayer seemed to call for this, it had not been mentioned).

The sermon delivered on this occasion is given on p.108 above.

---

[1] See "The Eucharistic Liturgy: Liturgical Expression on Convergence in Faith Achieved in Baptism, Eucharist and Ministry", introduced by Max Thurian, Geneva, WCC, 1983, esp. «Possible Simplifications", pp.11-14.

Entrance: Hymn

Roger Chapal: France

Pseulmes cinquante de David, Lyon, 1547

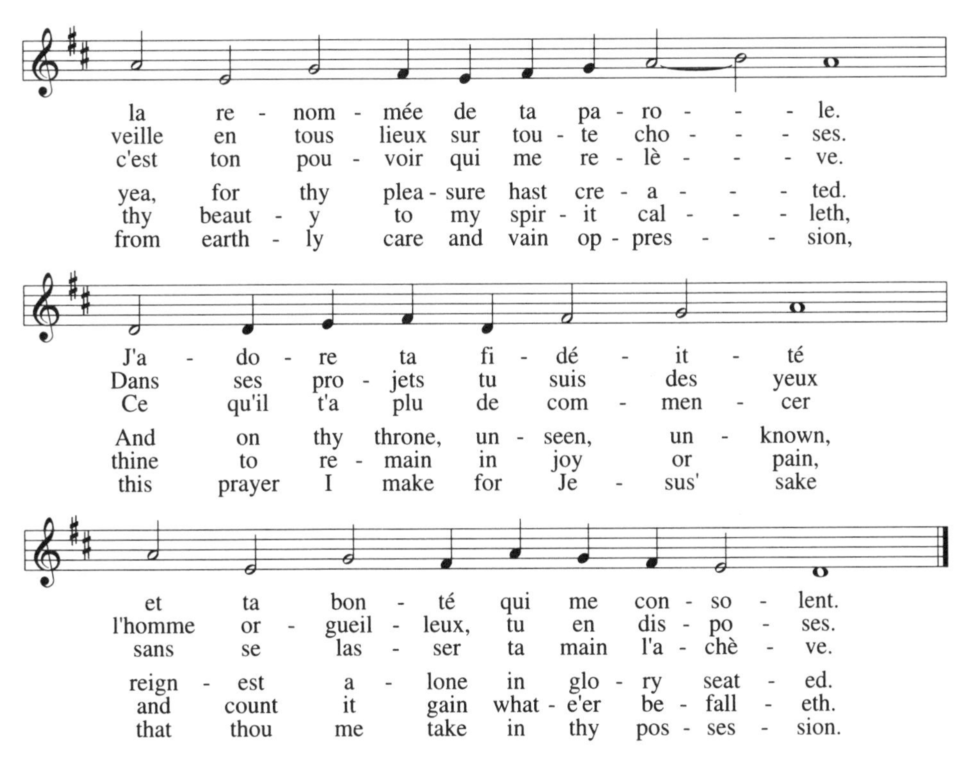

Greeting

P.: The grace of our Lord Jesus Christ,
the love of God,
and the communion of the Holy Spirit
be with you all.

C.: And also with you.

Confession

P.: Most merciful God,
we confess that we are in bondage to sin
and cannot free ourselves.
We have sinned against you.
We have not loved you with our whole heart;
we have not loved our neighbours as ourselves.
For the sake of your Son, Jesus Christ, have mercy on us.
Forgive us, renew us, and lead us,
so that we may delight in your will
and walk in your ways,
to the glory of your holy name.
Amen.

C.: Kyrie

G. M. Kolisi: South Africa

In 'ne-nce-ba' the middle syllable, 'nce,' is pronounced by making a 'tsch' sound that a mother uses to reprimand a child, with the addition of a nasalized beginning.

Absolution

P.: Almighty God have mercy on you, forgive you all your sins through our Lord Jesus Christ, strengthen you in all goodness, and by the power of the Holy Spirit keep you in eternal life.

C.: Amen.

Gloria

Luke 2:14

Pablo Sosa: Argentina

Collect

P.: Let us pray:
Lord God, gracious and merciful,
you anointed your beloved Son with the Holy Spirit
at his baptism in the Jordan,
and you consecrated him prophet, priest and king:
pour out your Spirit on us again
that we may be faithful to our baptismal calling,
ardently desire the communion of Christ's body and blood,
and serve the poor of your people and all who need our love,
through Jesus Christ, your Son, our Lord,
who lives and reigns with you,
in the unity of the Holy Spirit,
ever one God, world without end.

C.: Amen.

First reading

Alleluja

Gospel reading

Homily

Silence

Intercessions

O.: In faith let us pray to God our Father,
his Son Jesus Christ
and the Holy Spirit.
C.: O Lord, hear my prayer

Jacques Berthier: Taizé, France

O.: For the church of God throughout all the world,
let us invoke the Spirit.
C.: O Lord, hear my prayer

O.: For the leaders of the nations,
that they may establish and defend justice and peace,
let us pray for the wisdom of God.
C.: O Lord, hear my prayer

O.: For those who suffer oppression or violence,
let us invoke the power of the Deliverer.
C.: O Lord, hear my prayer

O.: That the churches may discover again their visible unity
in the one baptism which incorporates them in Christ,
let us pray for the love of Christ.
C.: O Lord, hear my prayer

O.: That the churches may attain communion
in the eucharist around one table,
let us pray for the strength of Christ.
C.: O Lord, hear my prayer

O.: That the churches may recognize each other's ministries
in the service of their one Lord,
let us pray for the peace of Christ.
C.: O Lord, hear my prayer
(spontaneous prayers of the congregation)

O.: Into your hands, O Lord,
we commend all for whom we pray,
trusting in your mercy;
through your Son, Jesus Christ, our Lord.
C.: Amen.

EUCHARIST

Preparation

O.: Blessed are you, Lord God of the universe,
you are the giver of this bread and this wine,
fruit of the earth and of human labour,
let it become the bread of life and the wine of the eternal kingdom.
As the grain once scattered in the fields
and the grapes once dispersed on the hillside
are now reunited on this table
in bread and wine,
so, Lord, may your whole church
soon be gathered together
from the corners of the earth into your kingdom.
C.: Blessed be God, now and forever!

Dialogue

P.: The Lord be with you
C.: And also with you.

P.: Lift up your hearts.
C.: We lift them to the Lord.

P.: Let us give thanks to the Lord our God.
C.: It is right to give him thanks and praise.

Preface

P.: Truly it is right and good to glorify you,
at all times and in all places,
to offer you our thanksgiving, O Lord, Holy Father,
Almighty and Everlasting God.
Through your living Word you created all things,
and pronounced them good.
You made human beings in your own image,
to share your life and reflect your glory.
When the time had fully come, you gave Christ to us
as the Way, the Truth and the Life.
He accepted baptism and announced the good news to the poor.
At the last supper
Christ bequeathed to us the eucharist,
that we should celebrate the memorial
of the cross and resurrection,
and receive his presence as food.
To all the redeemed Christ gave the royal priesthood
and, in loving his brothers and sisters,
chooses those who share in the ministry,
that they may feed the church with your word
and enable it to live by your sacraments.
Wherefore, Lord, with the angels and all the saints,
we proclaim and sing your glory:

Sanctus

The Iona Community: United Kingdom

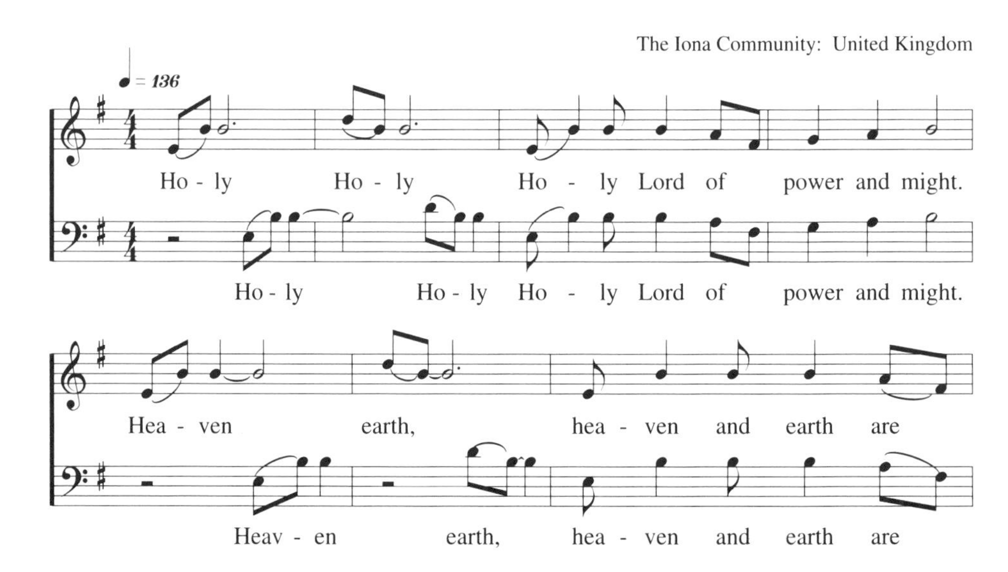

full of your glo - ry. All glo - ry to your name.
full of your glo - ry. All glo - ry to your
All glo - ry to your name, Bless - ed,
name. All glo - ry to your name, Bless - ed
bless– ed, is he who comes in the
Bless - ed is he who comes in the
name of the Lord. Bless - ed, bless– ed
name of the Lord. Bless - ed Bless - ed,
is he who comes in the name of the Lord. Ho - san - na in the
is he who comes in the name of the Lord
high - est. Ho - san - na in the high - est.
Ho - san-na in the high - est Ho - san-na in the high - est

Institution

P.: Almighty Father,
we thank you for the gift of your Son,
who, in the night in which he was betrayed,
took bread,
and when he had given thanks to you,
broke it and gave it to his disciples, saying:
Take, eat:
this is my body,
which is given for you.
Do this for the remembrance of me.
After supper he took the cup
and when he had given thanks,
he gave it to them and said:
Drink this, all of you:
this is my blood of the new covenant,
which is shed for you and for many
for the forgiveness of sins.
Do this for the remembrance of me.

Great is the mystery of faith.
C.: Your death, Lord Jesus, we proclaim!
Your resurrection we celebrate!
Your coming in glory we await!

Anamnesis

P.: Therefore, Lord,
we celebrate today the memorial of our redemption.

Epiclesis

P.: We ask you: Send your life-giving Spirit upon this eucharist,
so that this bread and wine may become for us the body and blood of Christ.
And as we partake of this body and blood,
fill us with the Holy Spirit
that we may be one single body and one single spirit in Christ.
C.: Amen.

Commemorations

O.: Remember, Lord,
your one, holy, catholic and apostolic church.
Reveal its unity, guard its faith.
Remember all the servants of your church:
bishops, presbyters, deacons,
and all to whom you have given special gifts of ministry,
together with your whole people.

Remember also all our sisters and brothers
who have died in the peace of Christ,
and those whose faith is known to you alone:
guide them to the joyful feast prepared
for all peoples in your presence.

C.: Maranatha, the Lord comes!

Conclusion

P.: Through Christ, with Christ, in Christ,
all honour and glory is yours,
Almighty God and Father,
in the unity of the Holy Spirit,
now and forever.

C.: Amen.

The Lord's prayer

O.: United by one baptism
in the same Holy Spirit and the same body of Christ,
we pray as God's sons and daughters:

C.: Our Father...

The peace

O.: Lord Jesus Christ, you told your apostles:
Peace I leave with you, my peace I give to you.
Look not on our sins but on the faith of your church;
In order that your will be done,
grant us always this peace
and guide us
towards the perfect unity
of your kingdom for ever

C.: Amen.

P.: The peace of the Lord be with you always

C.: And also with you.

P.: Let us give one another a sign of reconciliation and peace.

Lamb of God

C.: Lamb of God, you take away the sins of the world,
have mercy on us.
Lamb of God, you take away the sins of the world,
have mercy on us.
Lamb of God, you take away the sins of the world,
grant us peace.

Communion

Thanksgiving prayer

P.: In peace let us pray to the Lord:
O Lord, our God,
we give you thanks
for uniting us by baptism in the body of Christ
and for filling us with joy in the eucharist.
Lead us towards the full visible unity of your church
and help us to treasure all the signs of reconciliation
you have granted us.
Now that we have tasted of the banquet
you have prepared for us in the world to come,
may we all one day share together
the inheritance of the saints
in the life of your heavenly city,
through Jesus Christ, your Son, our Lord,
who lives and reigns with you
in the unity of the Holy Spirit,
ever one God, world without end.

C.: Amen.

Blessing

P.: The Lord bless you and keep you.
The Lord make his face to shine on you and be gracious to you.
The Lord look upon you with favour and give you peace.
Almighty God, Father, Son and Holy Spirit,
bless you now and forever.

C.: Amen.

Final hymn

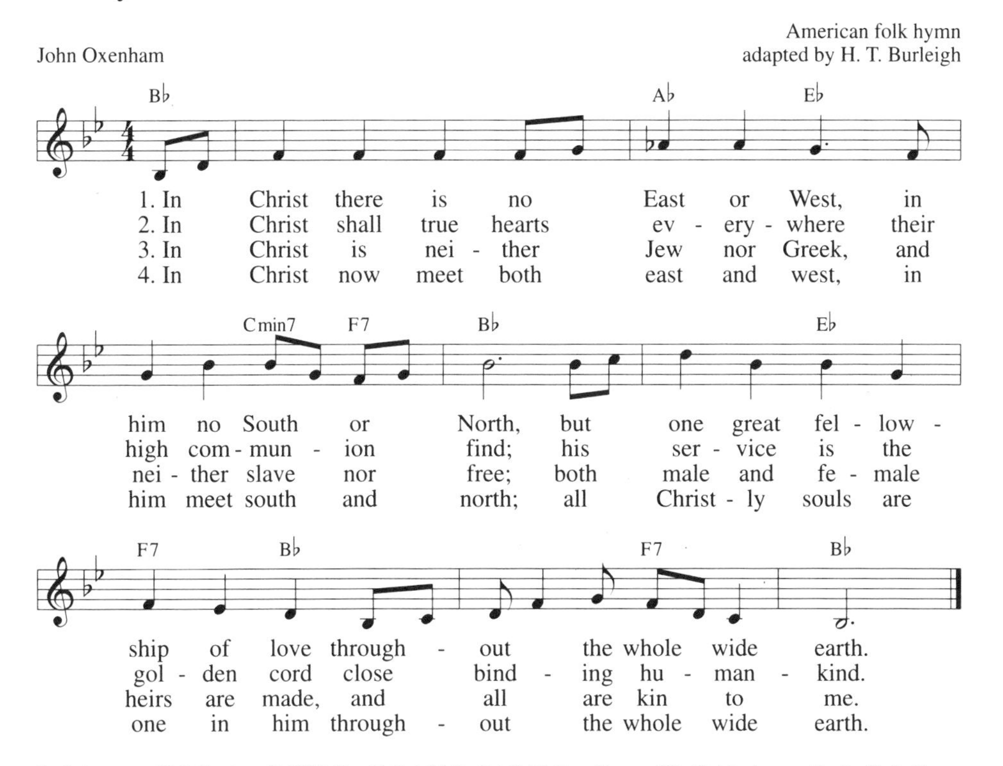
John Oxenham
American folk hymn
adapted by H. T. Burleigh
B♭
A♭
E♭
1. In Christ there is no East or West, in
2. In Christ shall true hearts ev - ery - where their
3. In Christ is nei - ther Jew nor Greek, and
4. In Christ now meet both east and west, in
Cmin7
F7
B♭
E♭
him no South or North, but one great fel - low -
high com - mun - ion find; his ser - vice is the
nei - ther slave nor free; both male and fe - male
him meet south and north; all Christ - ly souls are
F7
B♭
F7
B♭
ship of love through - out the whole wide earth.
gol - den cord close bind - ing hu - man - kind.
heirs are made, and all are kin to me.
one in him through - out the whole wide earth.

The Early-Morning Eucharist for Unity

Early each morning the Community of All Hallows celebrates the eucharist. A highlight during the consultation was the eucharist on Thursday morning, 25 August, the day when the sisters every week light a "candle for unity".[1] Some of the participants at the consultation were invited to contribute to this service through music (Korean, African, Latin American), preaching (the sermon is given on p.110 above) and taking other parts of the liturgy. In this way the traditional Anglican eucharist became a sign of unity, through the "inculturation" of music from other cultures.

The Mid-day Prayers

Taken as a whole, the five mid-day prayers reveal a special combination of unity in their general conception and structure, and variety in the way the individual services were developed. This variety was experienced as a great richness in the life of the consultation, and these services formed the most fruitful example of the possibilities of inculturation.

Each of these five daily worships was prepared and led by one of the participants, each of whom came from a different region. The leaders had been given the same basic order of worship, as printed below, and invited to develop a service using material coming particularly from their own tradition or region. They were free to choose songs and music, the psalm and the scripture reading, and whether they wanted to use fixed texts for intercessions or free prayer.

The intention was to have a consistent structure of mid-day worship each day, but within this to offer to one another the variety and richness of Christian worship as practised in different traditions and parts of the world. It was hoped also that this *unity-in-diversity* would provide a continuity and consistency which would help participants find some inner quiet.

Thus these worships illustrated an important aspect of the "liturgical renewal" which has occurred in many traditions since the 1950s, as the churches have recovered a

---

[1] During the consultation this custom was recommended for wider use as a form of prayer for Christian unity.

common understanding of the basic parts and general order of the service of the word. Our particular expression of this common worship pattern was taken, with some slight changes, from the *Book of Common Worship* of the Presbyterian Church (USA).[2]

Order for daily (mid-day) worship

— Opening sentences
— Hymn
— Psalm
— Short silence
— Scripture reading
— Silence for reflection on the meaning of the scripture reading
— Prayers of the people
— Lord's prayer
— Hymn
— Dismissal
— A sign of peace may be exchanged by all

Our experience was that although all the worship leaders kept to this proposed structure (with some minor variations), each daily worship was a distinct event with a character and special beauty of its own. The following texts of these five services show the variety and flexibility which is possible within the framework of a common worship order, and how worship materials from different traditions and regions can infuse this common pattern with their distinctive spirit.

Our experience was that the following aspects of the common worship order proved to be crucial in determining the distinctive character of each of the services:

— songs and music
— readings
— symbolic aspects, including visual symbols
— gestures and other symbolic actions
— clothing

[2] Louisville, Kentucky, Westminster/John Knox, 1993, p.544.

Monday, 22 August 1994

The first daily worship was prepared and led by Fr Milos Vesin (Serbian Orthodox, USA). A special act was the call to worship with the symbolic lighting of three candles in front of the altar. The music, mostly from the Orthodox tradition, gave its special atmosphere to the service. The focus was on repentance inspired by the commemoration of our common baptism.

Opening sentences

Leader: I will light a light in the name of the Father
who lit the world and breathed the breath of life into me.

I will light a light in the name of the Son
who saved the world and stretched out his hand to me.

I will light a light in the name of the Spirit
who encompasses my soul with yearning.

All: We will light three lights for the Trinity of love

Hymn — Hymn of Pentecost: Greece

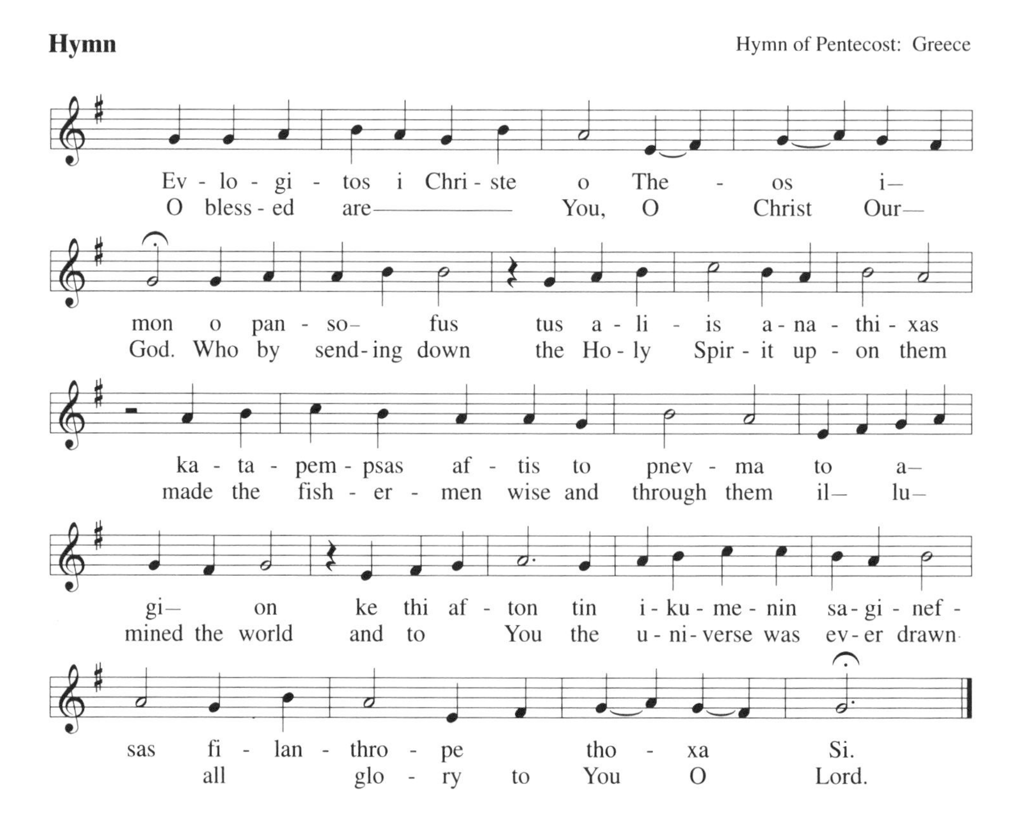

Prayer of confession

All: If we say we have no sin, we deceive ourselves and the truth is not in us. Trusting in God's mercy, we ask forgiveness for our sin.

Almighty God, you judge not by outward appearances and you know how often we turn away from you in thought, word and deed.

Forgive us and help us to live as your obedient sons and daughters.

Response

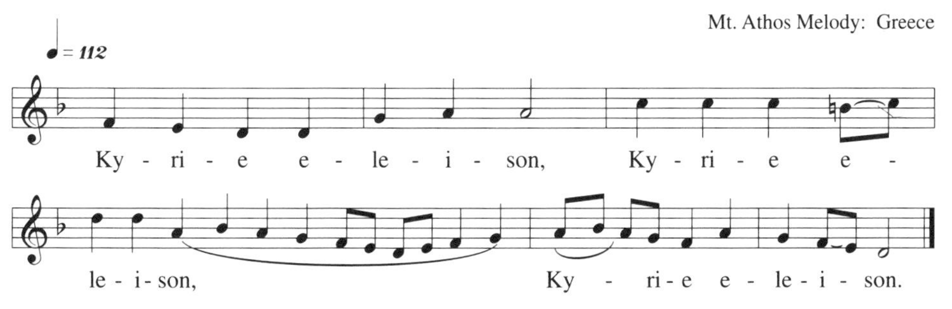

All: Loving Lord, friend of sinners and author of good news for the poor. Too often we neglect the needy and enjoy our freedom at the expense of others. Forgive us our pride, arrogance, and desire to dominate. Melt the hardness of our hearts and help us to love both neighbour and stranger.

Response: Kyrie…

L.: Christ gave himself for our sins.
I invite you to turn to your neighbour and say:
"May Jesus Christ give you grace and peace."

Sharing of peace

Song

Russia

Scripture reading: 1 Corinthians 10:1-4

Acclamation

All: We affirm and celebrate the increasing mutual recognition of one another's baptism as the one baptism into Christ.

We will dare to explore all the ways, known and unknown, to become one in Christ Jesus. We will not give up even in the face of difficulties.

Hymn

Lord's prayer

Benediction

L.: May God the Father who shared his love, strengthen us in our love for others. May the Son who shared his life grant us grace that we might share our life. And may the Holy Spirit indwelling us empower us to be only and always for others.

All: Amen

Hymn

Iona Community: Scotland

Noël Nouvelet: France

Tuesday, 23 August 1994

The second daily worship was prepared and led by Dr Young Sil Choi (Presbyterian, Korea). Its special character was introduced visually, with the leader wearing a traditional Korean costume. The scripture reading as well as other texts focused on issues of peace and justice. Through singing solo a traditional song, the leader drew attention to the special situation of Korea and its division into South and North.

Opening sentences

O God, you love justice and you establish peace on earth. We bring before you the disunity of today's world: the absurd violence, and the many wars, which are breaking the courage of the peoples of the world; militarism and the armaments race, which are threatening life on the planet; human greed and injustice, which breed hatred and strife.

Send your spirit and renew the face of the earth: teach us to be compassionate towards the whole human family; strengthen the will of all those who fight for justice and for peace; lead all nations into the path of peace, and give us the true koinonia in you which the world cannot give. Amen.

Response

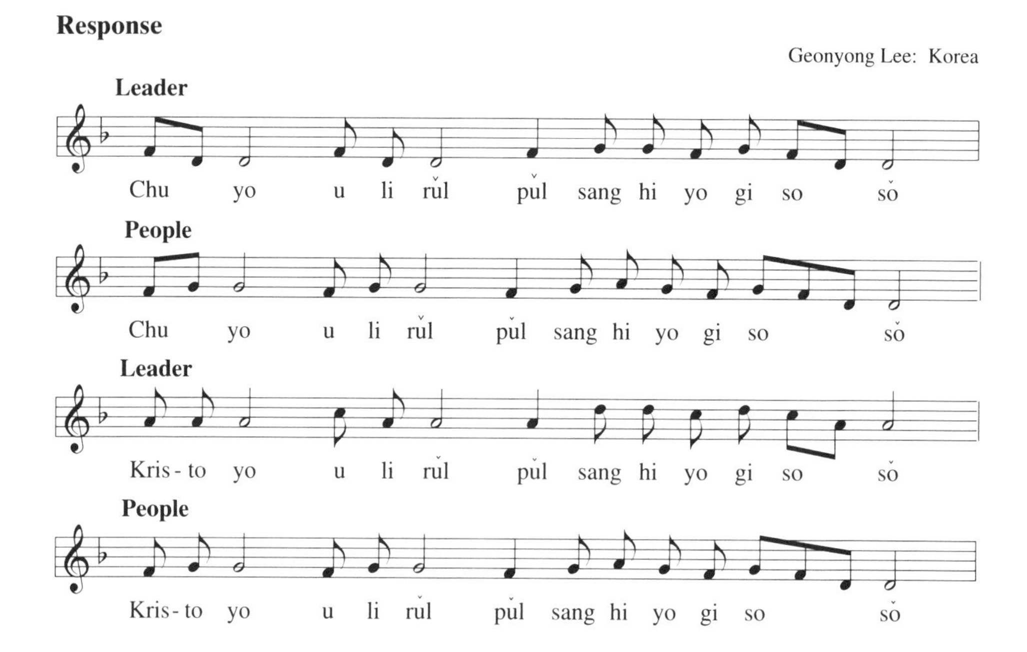

Lord have mercy. Christ have mercy. Lord have mercy.

Psalm: 85:8-13

Hymn

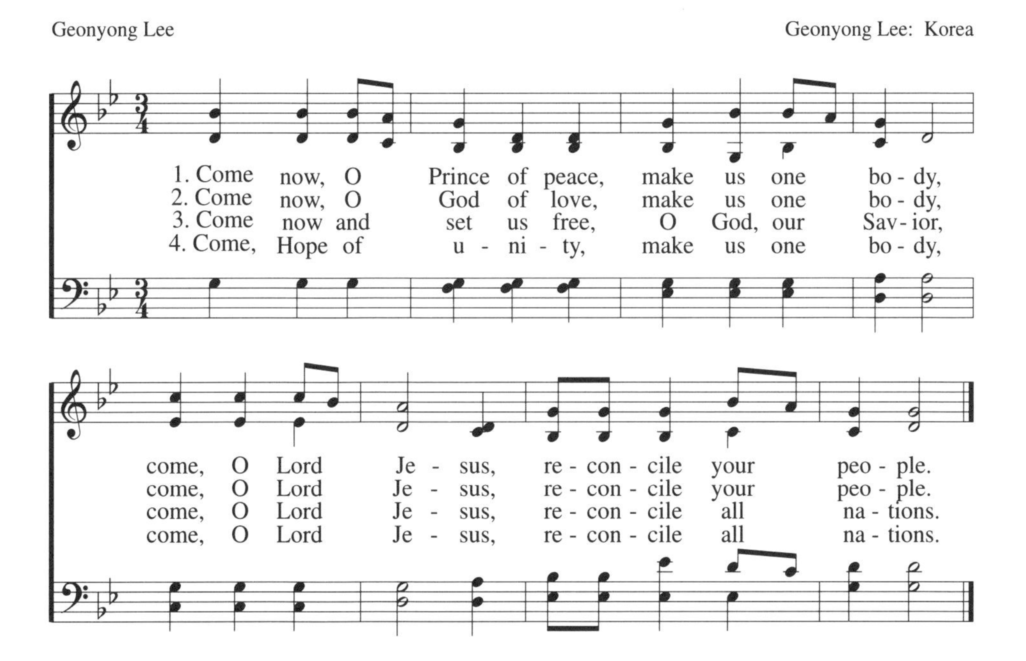

Reading: Ephesians 2:14-22

Short silence for reflection on the Bible reading

Prayer

Prayer 1 For peoples who are suffering in wars, racism, especially remembering peoples who are in Rwanda and Bosnia.

Prayer 2 For peoples who are in flight and who have to be separated from their family for all kinds of reasons, especially remembering peoples who are living in divided countries, refugees, and illegal immigrants.

Prayer 3 For women and children who are in tears and crying under the unjust and inhuman structure of society and the world, especially remembering poor women who are exploited economically and sexually in all continents of this world.

Prayer 4 For the repentance of peoples who are in power politically, militarily and economically.

Prayer 5 For the realization of true koinonia based on the cross of the sacrifice of Jesus Christ. And for the repentance of ourselves who are bound to egocentrism, racism, nationalism, localism, religious egotism. And for the giving of ourselves to our neighbours.

Lord's prayer (in our own language)

Peace

L.: Having all been made one through the sacrifice of our Lord.

P.: Let us make peace and justice in this world through laying down our lives for our neighbours.

(Let us offer one another a sign of peace)

Hymn

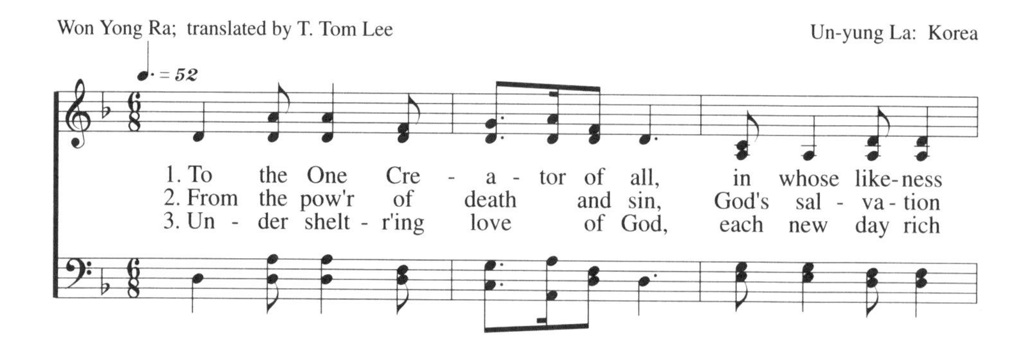

Blessing

L.: Now have in mind that we as Christians have the responsibility for koinonia.
P.: Yes. Amen.

L.: Go, with the intention to take care of justice, love and peace, with word and deed.
P.: Yes. Amen.

L.: Go, with the promise that you will meet Christ when you meet one of the least of your sisters and brothers.
P.: Yes. Amen.

L.: May God bless you and keep you.
May God's face shine upon you
and be gracious to you.
May God look upon you with kindness
and give you peace.
P.: Amen.

Wednesday, 24 August 1994

The third daily worship was prepared and led by Fr Emmanuel Badejo (Roman Catholic, Nigeria). Its special character was experienced especially through the lively African music — and the *movement* which goes with singing it! The focus coming from the scripture reading was Christian love.

Opening sentences

L.: In the name and presence of the Father, the Son and the Holy Spirit, we have been brought together in love. Let us unite our hearts and minds in prayer and ask for God's mercy.

All: Lord have mercy
Christ have mercy
Lord have mercy

L.: Come bless the Lord, all you who serve the Lord; who stand in the house of the Lord, in the courts of the house of our God.

Hymn

Scripture reading: Colossians 3:12-17

Responsorial psalm: (Response: Sing a new song to the Lord, He has done wonderful things) (Ps. 98)

Intercessions

All: Lord, hear our prayer.
— For church unity
— For the Pacific Islands
— For justice and peace
— For all present
— (Other intentions, silently)

All: The Lord's prayer (with hands open and arms raised)

All: Lord Jesus Christ, you said to your apostles: I give you peace, my peace I give you. Look not on our sinfulness but on the faith of your church and grant us the peace and unity of your kingdom, where you live forever and ever. Amen.

L.: Jesus Christ is our true peace, let us now share his peace with one another...

L.: Let us pray.

All: Father, creator of all that is good, you have called all men and women to work in your world and by their cooperation to better the condition of humanity. Grant to us a heart renewed that we may always work together as children of your family, and love all men and women as our brothers and sisters. Through Christ our Lord. Amen.

L.: Let us now go in peace singing and dancing to love and serve the Lord and our brothers and sisters.

All: Thanks be to God.

Hymn

as taught by Emmanuel Badejo: Nigeria

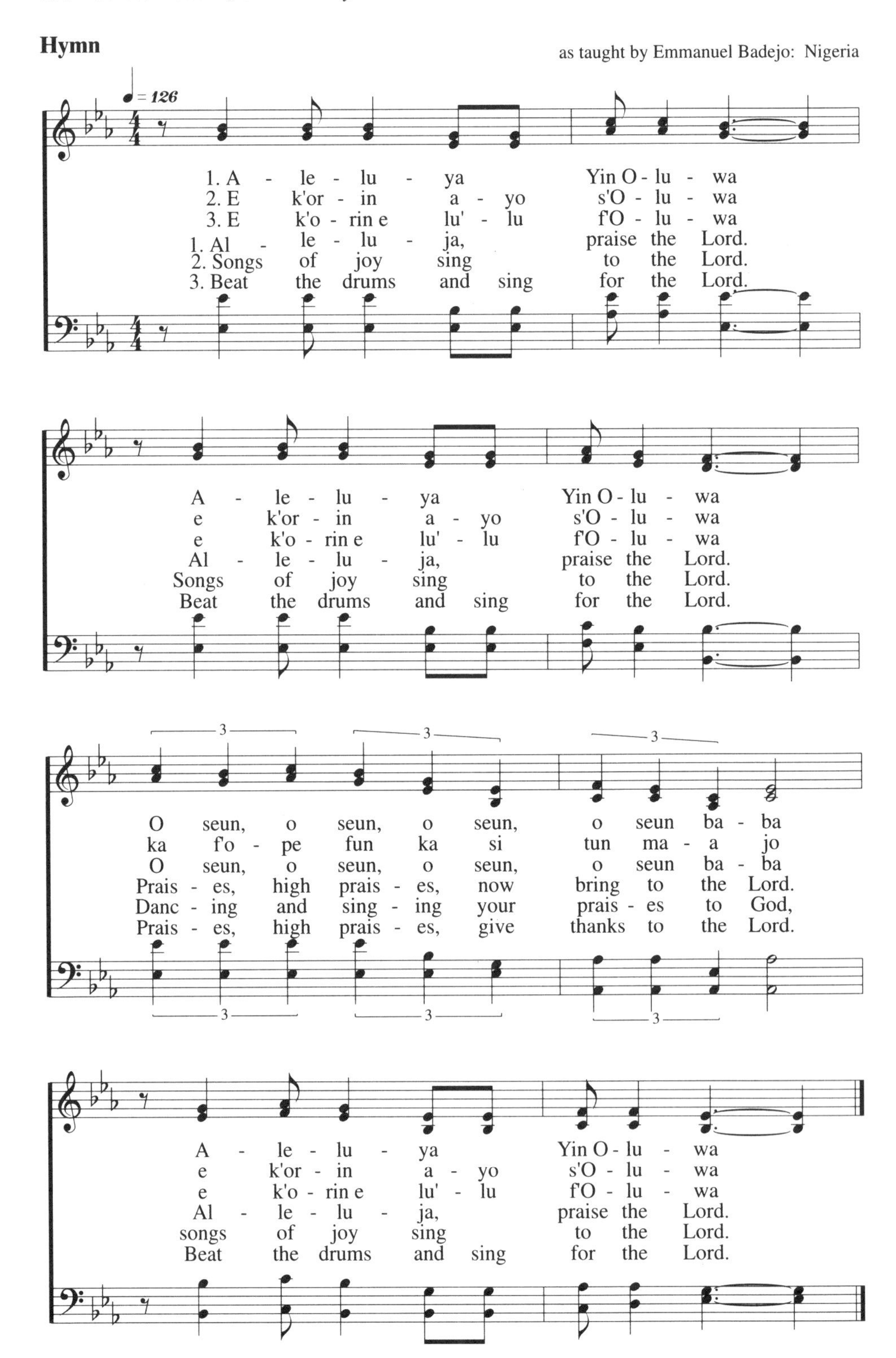

Thursday, August 25 1994

The fourth daily worship was prepared and led by Mrs Una Ratcliff (Roman Catholic, England). The opening sentences, as quotations from the Bible, were an exhortation while the scripture reading focused on the announcement of the Word becoming flesh. The mystery of God becoming human was the leading idea. A special sign was a procession at the end of the service to the altar where a candle symbolized the risen Christ. Persons bowed first in front of the cross at the wall, and then in front of the candle before leaving the sanctuary.

Opening sentences

1. The grace of our Lord Jesus Christ, the love of God and the fellowship of the Holy Spirit be with you all. (2 Cor. 13:14)
2. God is love, and those who live in love live in God and God lives in them. (1 John 4:16)
3. Try to grow perfect, help one another. Be united; live in peace, and the God of love and peace will be with you. (2 Cor. 13:11)
4. Just as a human body, though it is made up of many parts, is a single unit because all these parts, though many, make one body, so it is with Christ. In the one Spirit we were all baptized, Jews as well as Greeks, slaves as well as citizens, and one Spirit was given to us all to drink. (1 Cor. 12:12-13)
5. (My dear people) since God has loved us so much, we too should love one another. No one has ever seen God; but as long as we love one another God will live in us and his love will be complete in us. (1 John 4:11-12)

Hymn

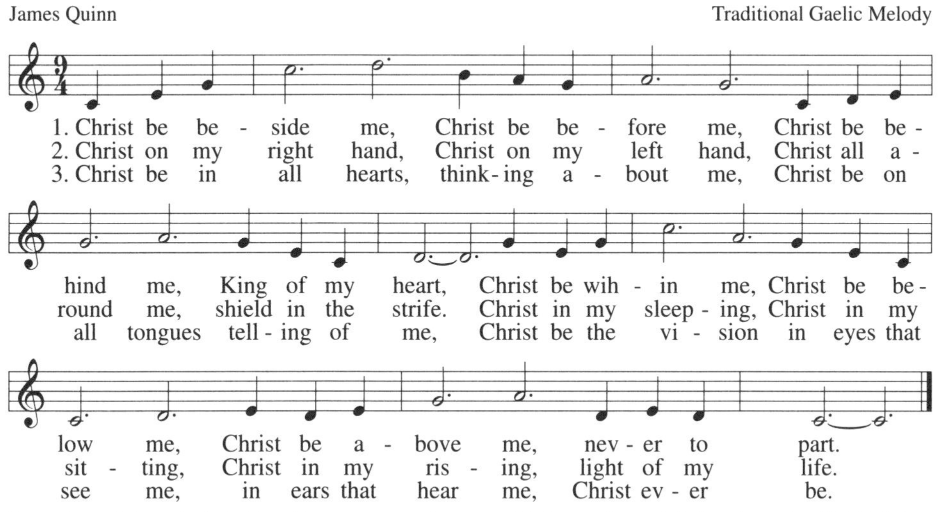

Psalm: 99

Short silence

Scripture reading: 1 John 1:1-7

Silence for reflection on the scripture reading

Prayers of the people:

L.: God our Father calls us to the perfection of communion, evoking within us a yearning to respond more fully to his will and to his infinite love, the love that is poured into our hearts through his Spirit. Let us turn to him with expectant faith as we express our special concerns at this time.

1. We pray that the signs of koinonia, a firm unwavering faith, the peace of reconciliation, a powerful Christian ministry, the apostolic teaching and sacramental life, may be evident in the church as Jesus stays with us always, even to the end of the world.

Response:

Jacques Berthier: Taizé, France

2. May the Holy Spirit guide us in this consultation, giving us wisdom, discernment and new insights in united worship. May he give us fresh understanding, leading us to consensus on issues which still divide us. May all Christians have the mind and heart of Christ, and attain the unity which is his will, so that the world may believe.
Response: O Lord, hear my prayer...

3. Two thousand and more islands in the Pacific Ocean come to mind as we bring them prayerfully to the Lord. We pray for the further spread of the gospel, increased unity among the churches, ecumenical councils and groups, and for ecumenical cooperation in tackling issues, including family problems, education and human development.
Response: O Lord, hear my prayer...

4. Before the cross of Christ, who suffered and died for us, we lift up to him the suffering people of our world — imprisoned, tortured, bereaved and fearful, hungry and homeless, sick and handicapped, spiritually, mentally or physically, and those lacking love in their lives. May Christ, who rose in glory, let his resurrection power touch them all, bringing courage, comfort and peace. May peace and justice become a reality in our world.
Response: O Lord, hear my prayer...

5. Christ is the light of the world: may his light of faith shine on those who do not yet know him, or those who have strayed from their commitment to him, and bring them peace and reconciliation.
Response: O Lord, hear my prayer...

6. We bring ourselves, just as we are, before the Lord, conscious of his loving care, asking him to meet our special needs and those of our families, friends, communities and churches.
Response: O Lord, hear my prayer...

L.: Uniting all our concerns, those spoken and those in our hearts, we pray as Jesus taught us:

The Lord's prayer

Dismissal

L.: May Almighty God bless us, keep us from all evil and bring us to everlasting life.

Sign of peace

L.: Let us go in peace to love and serve the Lord, and one another.

May Christ's peace permeate our hearts as we offer each other a sign of his peace.

Final hymn during procession

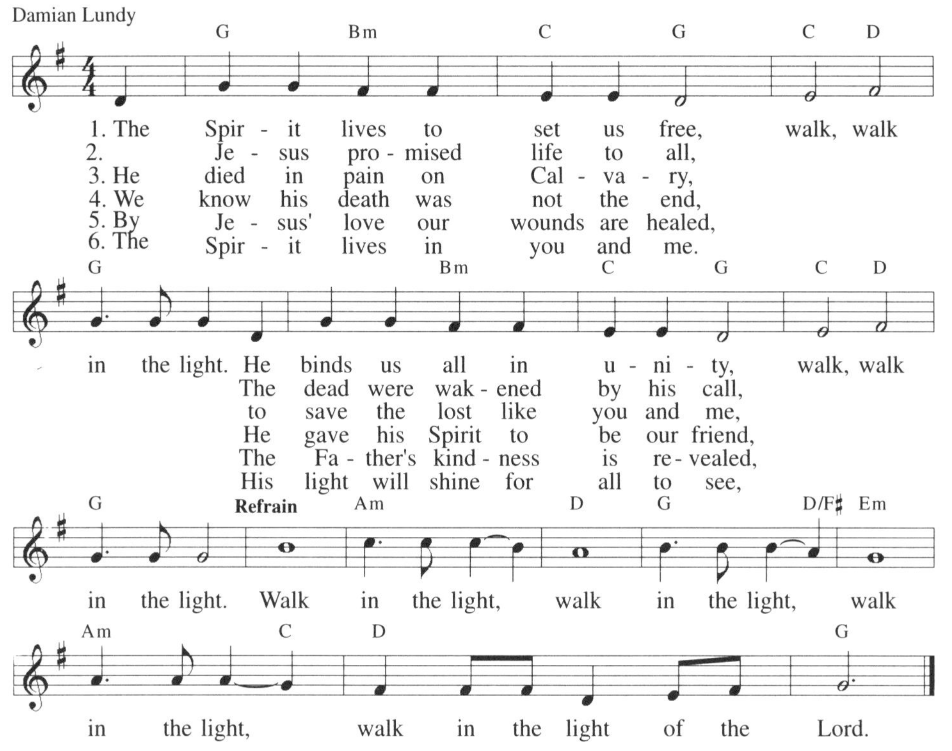

Friday, 26 August 1994

The fifth and last daily worship was prepared and led by Rev. César B. Gogorza (Lutheran, Argentina). It was held in Spanish (with English translation provided in the worship bulletin), and had a special emphasis on the intercessions. Participants came one by one to stand in the centre of the church, lighting an incense stick and offering intercessions (see the order of worship).

Introducción (Introduction)

L.: Queridos hermanas y hermanos: meditaremos en esta hora litúrgica sobre la intolerancia racial en el mundo. Especialmente, recordaremos los hechos ocurridos en Argentina.

(Dear sisters and brothers, during this time of prayer we shall reflect on racial intolerance in the world, especially the recent events in Argentina)

Los invito a cantar el primer himno. Escucharemos la melodia y luego cantaremos todos.

(I invite you to sing our first song. We shall listen to the melody and then we shall sing together)

Himno

2. Grenarna är många, stammen är en,
stammen - Jesus Kristus.
Grenarna är många, stammen är en,
vi är ett i honom.

3. Gåvorna är många, kärleken en,
finns i Jesus Kristus.
Gåvorna är många, kärleken en,
vi är ett i honom.

4. Tjänsterna är många, Anden är en,
Jesu Kristi Ande.
Tjänsterna är många, Anden är en,
vi är ett i honom.

5. Lemmarna är många, kroppen är en,
Jesu Kristi kyrka.
Lemmarna är många, kroppen är en,
vi är ett i honom.

2. Many are the branches of the one tree.
Our one tree is Jesus.
Many are the branches of the one tree.
We are one in Christ.

3. Many are the gifts giv'n, love is all one.
Love's the gift of Jesus.
Many are the gifts giv'n, love is all one.
We are one in Christ.

4. Many ways to serve God, the Spirit is one;
servant spirit of Jesus.
Many ways to serve God, the Spirit is one;
we are one in Christ.

5. Many are the members, the body is one;
members all of Jesus.
Many are the members, the body is one;
we are one in Christ.

2. Muchas son las ramas, un árbol hay:
y su tronco es Cristo.
Muchas son las ramas, un árbol hay
y en él somos uno.

3. Muchos son los dones, uno el amor:
el amor de Cristo.
Muchos son los dones, uno el amor
que nos hace uno.

4. Muchas las tareas, uno el sentir:
el sentir de Cristo.
Muchas las tareas, uno el sentir
que nos hace uno.

5. Muchos son los miembros, un cuerpo hay:
ese cuerpo es Cristo.
Muchos son los miembros, un cuerpo hay
y en él somos uno.

Salmo: Psalm 46

Silencio para reflexionar (silence for meditation)

Lectura de la palabra (scripture reading): 2 Corinthians 4:7-10

Reflexión silenciosa (silence for meditation)

Oración (prayer)

L.: Las oraciones serán armadas con las intensiones de cada uno en su propio idioma. A medida que compartimos nuestra intensión, cada uno prenderá un incienso y lo colocará en medio del círculo. Así como el humo y el perfume del incienso se mezclan para llenar el espacio, únanse nuestras oraciones hasta Dios, como señal de su Reino.

A cada intensión responderemos:

(Each of us can offer a prayer intention in her or his own language. While we share our intentions, we shall light an incense stick and put it in the centre of our circle. As the perfume and smoke of the incense mixes together, filling this room, let our prayers come together towards our God, as a sign of his kingdom.)

(To each intention we will answer:)

Response

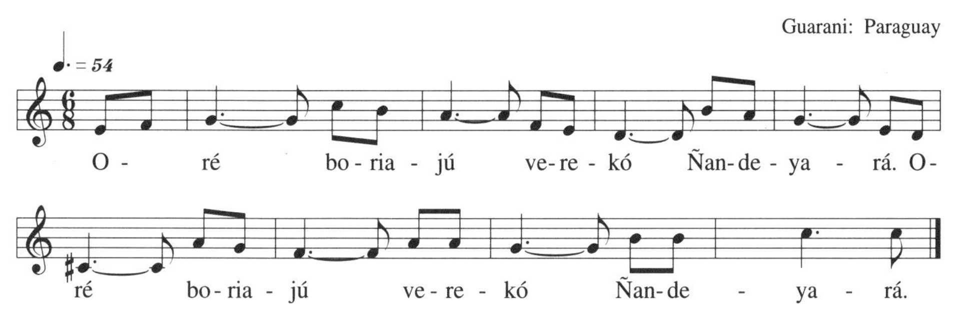

Lord, hear our prayer.

L.: Nos tomaremos de las manos para orar el Padrenuestro

(Let's hold hands to say the Lord's prayer)

Padrenuestro (Our father)

Himno

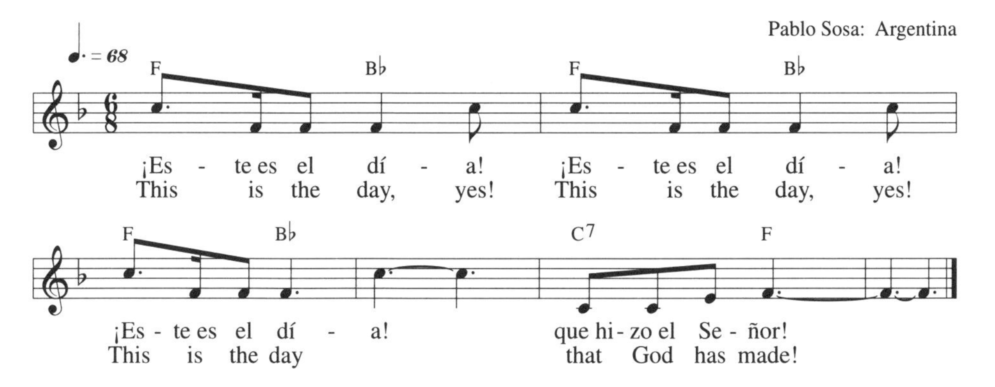

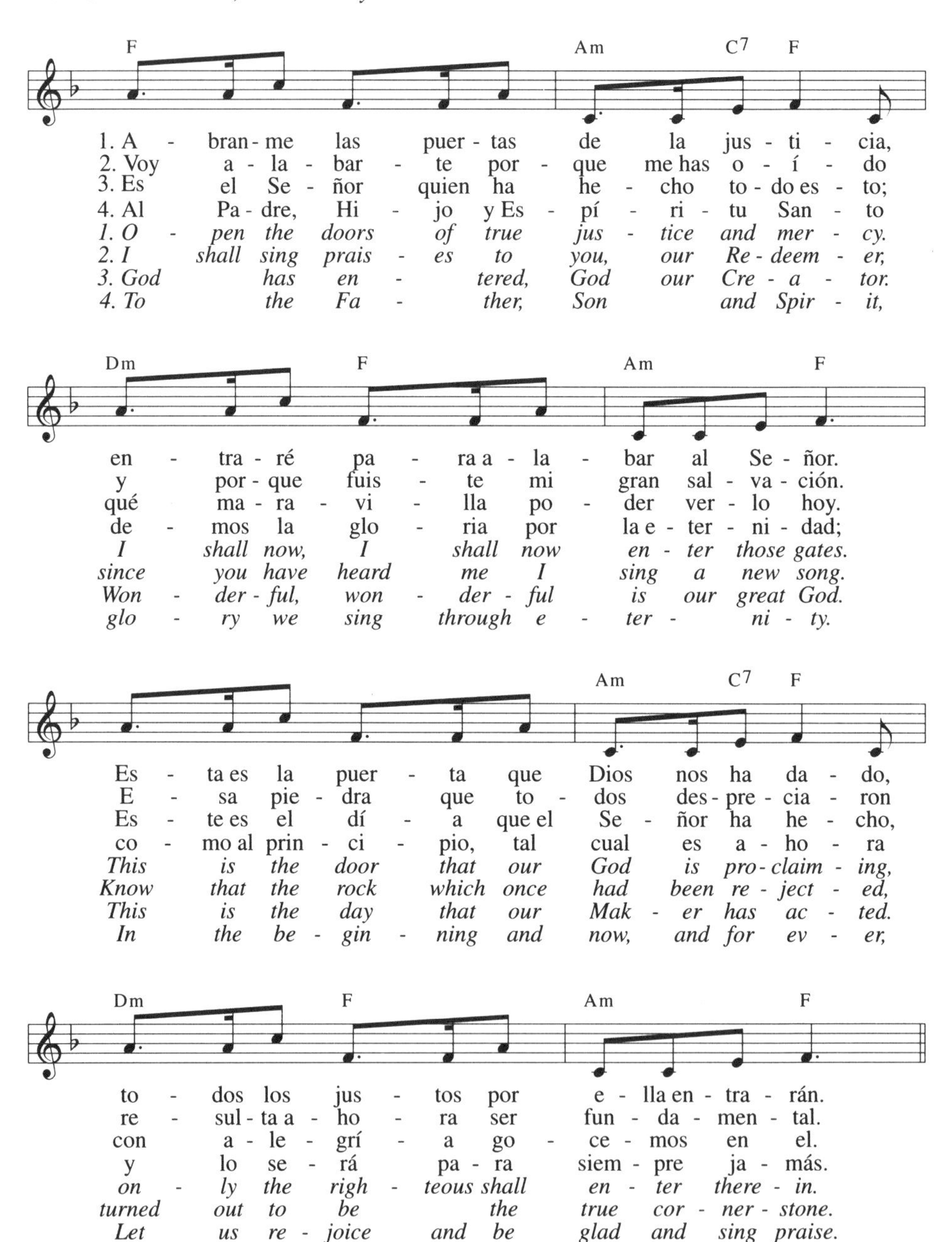

L.: El Señor todopoderoso nos bendiga, y dirija nuestros días y nuestros actos en su paz.

(The Lord Almighty bless us, and direct our days and deeds in his peace)

All: Amen.

The Closing Worship
26 August 1994

The closing worship was prepared and led by Fr Kwame Joseph Labi (Eastern Orthodox, Ghana). The worship was a "Service of the Blessing of the Bread" from the Orthodox tradition. This is a worship service with a symbolic action at its centre: the blessing of bread, wine, wheat and oil as well as the sharing of bread with the worshippers. It is specifically an Orthodox service, but is open to all. It should be emphasized that it is not a eucharistic service.

The fact that it was held in an Anglican chapel and with the mainly non-Orthodox participants of the consultation made this a significant example of an Orthodox worship conducted in an "ecumenical" situation. Although not held in a specifically Orthodox worship space, the words and actions of the service were meaningful to all those present.

We give here a basic structure for the service with some explanatory comments, together with some of the texts which were used.

Before the service, five loaves of bread, wheat, wine and oil had been placed on a stand in front of the congregation.

Blessing

Priest: Blessed is our God always now and for evermore.

Trisagion

(The "Thrice-Holy", a Byzantine hymn consisting of the invocation "Holy God, Holy Mighty, Holy Immortal, have mercy upon us", sung three times and followed by a doxology)

Lord's prayer

Psalm

Great litany

(Containing a number of intercessory biddings in alternation between the priest and the people, who answer, "Lord, have mercy")

Gospel reading: Matthew 14:14-21 (the feeding of the five thousand)

Intercessions

Blessing of the loaves, wheat, wine and oil

Priest: O Lord Jesus Christ our God, who didst bless the five loaves in the wilderness and didst satisfy the five thousand therewith, thyself bless these loaves, this wheat, wine and oil, and multiply them in this city, in the houses of those who celebrate this feast and in all thy world, and sanctify the faithful who partake of them. For it is thou who dost bless and sanctify all things, O Christ our God, and unto thee do we ascribe glory, together with thine unoriginate Father and thine all-holy and good and life-giving Spirit, now and ever, and unto ages of ages.

(The priest blesses the five loaves of bread, wheat, wine and oil)

Breaking of the bread

(The priest kisses the top loaf of bread and breaks it cross-wise)

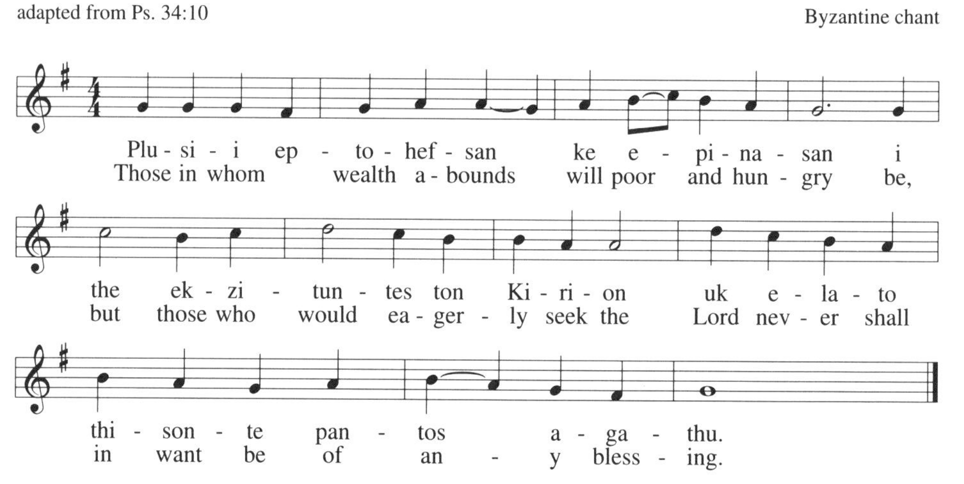

Blessing

Priest: The blessing of the Lord and his mercy come upon you through his divine grace and love towards mankind, always, now and ever, and unto ages of ages.

(After the priest blesses the congregation the people come forward and take a piece of bread. Dipping a finger in oil, they may trace on their forehead the sign of the cross.)

IV

Participants Contributors

Participants in the Consultation

Fr Emmanuel Badejo
(Roman Catholic)
Pontificio Collegio S. Pietro Apostolo
4, Vialle Mura Aurelie
00152 Rome
Italy

Rev. Dr Sebastian Bakare
(Anglican)
University of Zimbabwe
Box MP 167
Mount Pleasant, Harare
Zimbabwe

Prof. Young Sil Choi
(Presbyterian)
St Michael's Theological College
Kuro-Ku, Hang Dong 1-1
Seoul
Korea

Fr Anscar Chupungco, O.S.B.
(Roman Catholic)
Paul VI Institute of Liturgy
PO Box 18, Malaybalay
The Philippines

Rev. Janet Crawford (Moderator)
(Anglican)
St John's College, Private Bag 28 907
Remuera, Auckland 1136
New Zealand

Rev. Hugh Cross
(Baptist)
c/o Church of Christ the Cornerstone
300, Saxon Gate West
Central Milton Keynes MK9 2ES
England

Rev. Dr Colin Davey (24-25/8)
(Anglican)
Inter-Church House, 35-41 Lower Marsh
London SE 1 7RL
England

Dr Sophie Deicha
(Eastern Orthodox)
50, rue de Mareil
78100 St Germain-en-Laye
France

Prof. Dr Kyriaki FitzGerald
(Eastern Orthodox)
43, ch. Moïse-Duboule
1209 Geneva
Switzerland

Rev. Dr Thomas FitzGerald
(Eastern Orthodox)
Unit I, World Council of Churches
150, route de Ferney
1211 Geneva 2
Switzerland

Rev. César B. Gogorza
(Lutheran)
Diagonal 73 N 941
La Plata, Pcia de Buenos Aires
Argentina

Rev. Robert Gribben
(United)
Wesley Uniting Church
148 Lonsdale Street
Melbourne, Vic. 3000
Australia

Canon Prof. David Holeton
(Anglican)
Trinity College
Toronto M5S 1H8
Canada

Rev. Fr Kwame Joseph Labi
(Eastern Orthodox)
P.O. Box 274
Legon
Ghana

Rev. Prof. Gordon Lathrop
(Lutheran)
Lutheran Theological Seminary
7301 Germantown Ave
Philadelphia, PA 19119
USA

Rev. Dr Prof. Jaci Maraschin
(Anglican)
Rua Rega Freitas 530, F-13
01220-010 Sao Paulo, SP
Brasil

Rev. Rodney Matthews
(Baptist)
36A Llanthewy Road
Newport, Gwent NP9 4LA
United Kingdom

Rev. Dr Samuel Mwaniki
(Presbyterian)
P.O. Box 48268
Nairobi
Kenya

Rev. Dr Kjell O. Nilsson
(Lutheran)
Christian Council of Sweden
Box 1764
111 87 Stockholm
Sweden

Mother Pamela C.A.H.
(Anglican)
All Hallows Convent, Ditchingham
Bungay, Suffolk, NR35 2DT
England

Preacher Richard Phua
(Presbyterian)
Orchard Road Presbyterian Church
Orchard Road
Singapore 0923
Republic of Singapore

Dr Samson Prabhakar
(United)
United Theological College
63 Miller's Road
Bangalore 560 046
India

Mrs Una Ratcliff
(Roman Catholic)
42, Winchelsea Avenue
Bexleyheath, Kent DA7 5HP
England

Rev. Fr Jorge Scampini
(Roman Catholic)
Convento Santo Domingo
Defensa 422
1065 Buenos Aires
Argentina

Oberkonsistorialrat Dr Matthias Sens
(United)
Evangelisches Konsistorium
Am Dom 2, Postfach 122
39104 Magdeburg
Germany

Rev. Anita Stauffer
(Lutheran)
Lutheran World Federation
150, route de Ferney
1211 Geneva 2
Switzerland

Fr Milos Vesin
(Eastern Orthodox)
St Archangel Michael
Serbian Orthodox Church
9815 Commercial Avenue
Chicago, IL 60617
USA

Rt Rev. Dr Zacharias Mar Theophilus
(Mar Thoma)
Santhi Giri, II/488 Edathala North
Alwaye 683564, Kerala
India

Staff

Rev. Dr Thomas F. Best
(Disciples of Christ)
Faith and Order, Unit I, WCC

Mrs Eileen Chapman
(Presbyterian)
Faith and Order, Unit I, WCC

Rev. Dr Dagmar Heller
(United)
Faith and Order, Unit I, WCC

Rev. Terry MacArthur
(Methodist)
WCC Worship Consultant, Unit I, WCC

Contributors to This Volume

Janet Crawford teaches church history and liturgics in the College of St John the Evangelist within the Auckland Consortium for Theological Education, New Zealand. She is a member of the Faith and Order Commission.

Gordon Lathrop is the Schieren professor of liturgy and chaplain at the Lutheran Theological Seminary at Philadelphia, USA. He is a past president of the North American Academy of Liturgy and a member of the editorial board of the journal *Worship*.

Thomas FitzGerald is executive director of Unit I: Unity and Renewal, World Council of Churches.

Anscar J. Chupungco, O.S.B., is head of the Pontifical Liturgical Institute, Rome, and of the Paul VI Institute of Liturgy, Bukidnon, The Philippines.

S. Anita Stauffer is study secretary for worship, Department for Theology and Studies of the Lutheran World Federation, Geneva.

Jaci Maraschin is professor at the Ecumenical Institute of Post-Graduate Studies on Sciences of Religion, São Paulo, Brasil.

Samuel Mwaniki is the secretary general of the Presbyterian Church of East Africa, Kenya.

Samson Prabhakar is professor of Christian ministry at United Theological College, Bangalore, India.

Sophie Deicha is professor at Institut de théologie orthodoxe Saint-Serge, Paris, France.

Hugh Cross is ecumenical moderator, Milton Keynes Christian Council, Milton Keynes, England.

Rodney Matthews is a Baptist minister who for twenty years has helped to produce ecumenical liturgical texts on baptism, eucharist and ministry as part of the growth towards a uniting church in Wales.

Zacharias Mar Theophilus is the bishop in charge of ecumenical relations and theological education for the Mar Thoma Syrian Church, India. He is a member of the WCC central and executive committees.

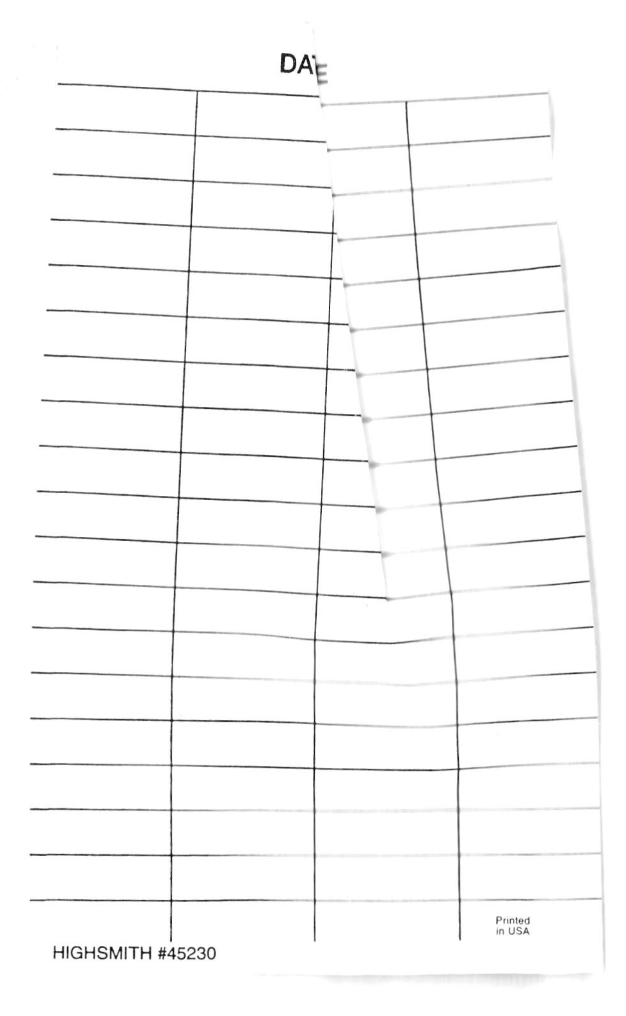
DA
HIGHSMITH #45230
Printed in USA